When Bad Things Happen to Good Quilters

A GUIDE TO STARTING, FIXING, AND FINISHING YOUR QUILTING PROJECTS

Joan Ford

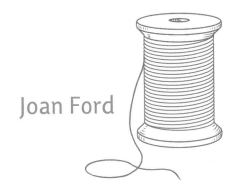

The Taunton Press

This work is dedicated to Karen, my niece. She caught the quilty "bug" while making her very first quilt block only recently. Even though many miles separate us, we managed to share her first quilt project, start to finish, together.

The Taunton Press
Inspiration for hands-on living®

The Taunton Press, Inc., 63 South Main Street, PO Box 5506, Newtown, CT 06470-5506
e-mail: tp@taunton.com

Executive editor: Shawna Mullen
Assistant editor: Tim Stobierski
Technical editor: Jodie Davis
Copy editor: Betty Christiansen
Indexer: Barbara Mortenson
Original cover design: Alison Wilkes
Cover illustrator: Peter Horjus
Original interior design: First edition design by 3+ Co.; revised and updated edition design
    by Rita Sowins/Sowins Design
Interior illustrators: William Michael Wanke and Joan Ford
Layout: Rita Sowins/Sowins Design
Layout coordinator: Amy Griffin
Photographers: Burçu Avsar (p. 51, 53, 56); all others, Scott Phillips

The following names/manufacturers appearing in *When Bad Things Happen to Good Quilters* are trademarks: Band-Aid®, Kwik Klip™, Quiltsmart®, Velcro®, Wisk®, ZigZapps!™

Library of Congress Cataloging-in-Publication Data

Ford, Joan, 1961-
  When bad things happen to good quilters : survival guide for fixing & finishing any quilting project / author, Joan Ford.
    pages cm
  Includes index.
  ISBN 978-1-62710-393-0
1. Quilting. 2. Patchwork--Patterns. 3. Quilts--Repairing. I. Title.
  TT835.F66773 2014
  746.46--dc23
                    2014037710

Note: The templates in this book may be copied and enlarged for personal use only.

Acknowledgments

Quilts are so much more than fabric, batting, and thread. Quilting is one of those things that you shouldn't do if you don't fully enjoy every single minute of it. And when bad things happen to any of us, a dark shadow appears. It's my hope that this book offers advice, solutions, and a chuckle or two that will chase those occasional shadows away. Thank you, dear quilter, for embracing a hobby that offers a universe of possibilities.

Thank you also to the quilt shop owners who open their doors every day. They sell fabric, thread, and patterns, but also offer inspiration and excitement to all who venture inside.

For me, like a quilt and its component parts, this book represents so much more than the paper it's printed on. It is the physical compilation of the talents of an entire collaborative, creative team of amazing people. From cover to cover, swarms of people have read, edited, advised, supported, cheered, checked, altered, absorbed, and improved this book in ways that cannot be quantified. For these many hands, sharp eyes, and inspiring commentary, I am truly grateful. Special thanks to the phenomenal editorial staff at The Taunton Press, especially Maria Taylor, Shawna Mullen, and Tim Stobierski, for their boundless encouragement and ongoing support—and to the many, many behind-the-scenes players without whom this book really would be a stack of blank pages: many, many thanks.

Contents

Introduction

Three simple letters: UFO. Say these three letters in that sequence to nearly any experienced quilter, then step back and watch the fireworks.

A full range of possible reactions will follow: horror, guilty laughter, rolling eyes, fear, disgust, outright giddiness. What does it mean? To a quilter, those three letters mean, almost universally, UnFinished Object(s).

So, if this is to be a book about bad things that happen to good quilters, why start with a discussion about unfinished projects? It's my theory that a project gets to be a UFO because something went wrong.

It could be very early in the process. You choose a pattern and then can't find the exact fabrics that made you fall in love in the first place, so you choose different fabrics. Maybe one of the fabrics you've selected throws things off the tiniest bit, and your heart just doesn't sing anymore. The project lands on the shelf-to-nowhere, doomed to UFO status.

Or maybe it happened somewhere in the middle. The project is clipping along, and the instructions throw you for a curve. An unfamiliar technique, a mistake in the pattern, too much math. Now you have to think, and scratching your head this much, even for your favorite quilting hobby, isn't very fun. The project goes onto the infamous shelf, unfinished, waiting for another day when your brain is up for a challenge.

Or you can fall out of love because you made an obvious mistake that needs fixing—it's not one of those issues that can be overlooked. It means backward progress when you want to be moving forward. The shelf gains another victim.

We are quilters. When bad things happen, we don't want to give up, but sometimes we *move on*, if only temporarily, hoping that the problem will fix itself. But problems don't fix themselves. Sometimes a little help is all you need to get the projects past the problem and off the shelf, onto your "Ta-Done" list.

This book offers just that—a little advice to help you resolve all those pesky little setbacks and get your quilty projects back on track.

Don't expect this book to offer encyclopedic knowledge on all things quilty, because you won't find that here. What you'll find is more practical: a collection of ideas, different perspectives, and suggestions to get your projects past the snags and into existence—with a little humor, of course, to remind you why quilting became your favorite hobby in the first place.

There is nothing particularly difficult about quilting as long as you approach each step as it comes, deal with issues as they arise, and forge ahead. The answer is always out there, though sometimes you might have to dig a little deeper to see it or get some advice from a trusted friend. And here I am!

So gather your quilty tools, step up to the cutting counter, fire up the iron, flip the switch on the sewing machine, and make sure your studio chair seat back is set in the full upright position—getting to the Land of Finished Quilts might sometimes make for a bumpy ride, but with a little determination, a chuckle here and there, and a bit of "stick-tuition," success is at hand.

When bad things happen to good quilters . . . good quilters get sewing!

A Bonus Project Just for You!

In addition to the 4 projects at the end of this book, I've created another one to help you practice your quilty skills. Visit www.taunton.com/GoodQuilters to download the Seeing Stars Quilt.

 Beth's Treat

My friend Beth loves to buy fabric—and kits and patterns—not because she needs it, but because she loves it. She's a collector, and her fabric storage area is a source of envy. At last count, she has more than 60 unfinished quilt projects, and each one is special. To stay on the finish line and off the starting block, she has devised a system to keep her urge to purchase new quilting projects under control.

Nearly every quilter has a collection of pincushions, and Beth has chosen two special pincushions for only one purpose—to determine when she's allowed a new fabric treat.

Her system is simple: She places a certain number of pins on one pincushion, the *intention* pincushion. Each pin represents one UFO from her stash. She starts with as many as 12 pins on this cushion. The pin moves to the second pincushion, representing *success*, only after the UFO it represents is complete.

Once the success pincushion accepts all the fancy pins from the intention pincushion, Beth allows herself to purchase *one* new project. She may purchase new fabrics before all the pins have moved to the success pincushion only if the new fabrics will be used to complete one of the UFOs.

It's a great system! Beth is usually very disciplined about staying on track and moving the beautiful pins one at a time. As more pins move to the receiving pincushion, she begins to plan her treat purchase.

But Beth will be the first to admit that the system has its flaws. A stressful event on a busy day in the office, paired with a soul-soothing trip to the quilt shop, can spoil the best-laid pincushion planning. Like so much else in quilting, the system is all about discipline!

Hardware

You'd be surprised how many quilty emergencies can be avoided just by making sure you understand your tools. Are they appropriate for the job at hand? Are they working? Could you be using them better?

All the Right Stuff

Any cook knows that even if you have the best cuts of meat, the freshest vegetables, and the tastiest spices, you won't get very far making a meal without pots, pans, utensils—and a tried-and-true recipe.

Of course, you can always call the local takeout restaurant and order some positively yummy pizza—but it's never quite as satisfying as the homemade variety, the kind you make from scratch in your own kitchen, infused with the best ingredients and a heaping amount of love.

Like the pizza, I suppose you can buy a quilt, but how much fun is that? Just think how satisfying it is to make your very own quilt from start to finish. And it's easy: Like making the pizza, it has a step-by-step process, with tons of room for variety.

As with a delicious homemade pizza, once you've made one quilt, it's hard to stop. Some good choices on basic tools will make your life and your hobby a whole lot easier and more fun. Here's where it gets a little tricky. With so many alternatives available to today's sewist, it's hard to narrow them down. Let's examine some of the possibilities and pitfalls of each choice.

The Sewing Machine Is Your Friend

A sewing machine in good working condition just might be the most critical element in determining how much you enjoy quilting. If the machine is working properly, there is harmony in the sewing room.

New sewing machine models are introduced every year, with all kinds of shiny, high-tech features and improvements. But all of that technology can come at a price. With so many different brands and models of sewing machines available, you'd need a book the size of an encyclopedia to evaluate all the possible things a sewing machine can do.

To make a good companion for quilting, a sewing machine should have a few key features:

- A ¼-in. foot, with or without a guide. Most piecing is done using a scant ¼-in. seam (see p. 38 for more details)

- Needle-up, needle-down capability

- Left/right needle position adjustment

- Feed dogs that can be lowered

- Upper thread tension adjustment

- Stitch length adjustment

- A few decorative stitches, especially zigzag and blanket stitch or buttonhole stitch

- An easy-to-access bobbin case

COMMON SEWING MACHINE FEET USED FOR QUILTING

¼-in. foot	For piecing
Walking foot	For straight-line quilting or extra-bulky materials
Open-toe foot	For decorative stitches, machine appliqué
Darning foot or free-motion quilting foot	For free-motion quilting (the curvy, squiggly stuff)
Zipper foot	For attaching zippers or piping
Buttonhole foot	For adding a button to a project

In addition to the previous essentials, there are a lot of nice-to-have optional features, like hand controls that allow you to disengage the foot pedal and start and stop the sewing machine motion with the press of a button (this is particularly nice for free-motion quilting). A freehand system or knee lift to simultaneously raise the presser foot and drop the feed dogs, *bobbin-low* or *bobbin-out* alerts, a stitch regulator, or special stitches for quilting can also be helpful.

If you are purchasing a new machine for your quilting hobby, buy a machine that fits your budget and feels right for your abilities. A nicely formed straight stitch on a machine that is easy to use and maintain is important. But even more crucial is a service department you can depend on. Before you buy any sewing machine, test-drive the machine and understand its features, and ask the sewing machine dealer how service is handled.

 The Dreaded Thread Cutter

Notice that an automatic thread cutter didn't make my list of sewing machine gotta-haves. I've owned several sewing machines with an automatic thread cutter, and I rarely use it because I don't like the severed threads on the underside of the piecework or quilt, and I can control the thread ends better if I can see them.

Change Is Good

When the sewing machine simply isn't working properly, something as basic and inexpensive as a fresh needle could be the easy remedy.

I turned to industry expert Rhonda Pierce, marketing director for Euro-Notions and schmetzneedles.com, for some advice on when to change your needle. Rhonda says:

"The rule of thumb is to change the needle after eight hours of sewing, but we use different techniques, on different fabrics with various finishes and dyes, in different sewing environments, and we sew at different speeds. With all these variables, changing the needle every eight hours may be too frequent or not enough. So far, I have heard from only one power quilter who changed the needle every four hours! When sewing, quilting, or embroidering, we should be in our groove—in tune with our machine as fabric, thread, and needle do a stitch dance. Your sewing machine will talk to you with these clues to change the needle:

- Broken or shredded thread
- Skipped or uneven stitches
- Puckered or damaged fabric
- Popping or clunking sounds made by the sewing machine

"When in doubt, switch to a fresh needle. It's a minimal investment with big payoff potential."

THINGS THAT GO "BUMP"

If your machine isn't running smoothly, it can completely ruin a perfectly good sewing session. If a problem arises, it can be frustrating beyond words. A few simple adjustments can make all the difference.

NAME THAT LINT BUNNY

If you remove the needle plate and discover a felt mat covering the bobbin case—no, that's not supposed to be there—grab the lint brush. With the brush, gently remove the monster lint bunny that has taken up residence in the machine. He's fuzzy and very colorful, but he's keeping the sewing machine from doing its job. Imagine putting on three heavy sweaters, a down coat, two pairs of gloves, and fluffy mittens. Then try to thread a needle. That's what you are asking your sewing machine to do!

As long as you have the brush handy, brush the lint away from the needle bar, the metal bar that holds the sewing machine needle. Pay particular attention to where the needle bar passes through the sewing machine cover.

GREASE IS THE WORD

While that needle plate is off, add a dot of sewing machine oil every third or fourth bobbin change to keep things running smoothly. Refer to your sewing machine manual for specific instructions. Where you place the drop of oil can vary from machine to machine. Your sewing machine will thank you with smooth movements, even stitches, and reduced thread breakage.

After adding oil, especially if you are using light-colored thread or light-colored fabric, take about a half-dozen waste stitches on a fabric scrap. Without this step, the fresh oil will transfer to the thread, and to your project, but only for the first few stitches.

TWO TENTS? OR TOO TENSE?

A slight thread tension adjustment can do wonders for sewing machine performance, especially when you are switching from piecing to quilting and back again. Usually, the rule us to increase the upper thread tension when moving from piecing to quilting, and decrease the upper thread tension when moving back from quilting to piecing. Sew a test seam or quilt a few stitches on a small quilt sandwich if you aren't familiar with the sewing machine upper thread tension settings that work best on your machine.

To test thread tension, set the straight stitch to a 4x4 setting—stitch length and width both set to 4. If your machine settings don't go this high, set the machine to a large zigzag, then sew. Under ideal tension settings, this should produce well-formed, equal stitches on the top and just the smallest, tiniest loop on either end of the stitch from the bottom.

For quilting, especially free-motion quilting, check the underside of the quilt as you start quilting a new project. Start quilting as you normally would, then stop when you have a quilting line about 6 in. to 10 in. long. Make sure the needle is in the *needle down* position,

then take a peek at the underside of the quilt. If you notice some issues with the stitch formation, an adjustment may be needed. Increase the upper thread tension if you see thread loops that look a little like spider legs, especially around free-motion curves.

From the top of the quilt, if you notice dots of bobbin thread in the stitches, a slight decrease in the upper thread tension may help.

Dots showing in between stitches on the top of the quilt may be fixed with a slight decrease in upper thread tension.

If you really aren't sure about the thread tension, before diving into your quilt project, make a test quilt sandwich, about 10 in. square, out of two scraps of fabric with batting in between. If possible, use materials that are similar to the fabrics in the quilt. Make the test line of sewing and check the underside of the test sandwich. If you encounter tension problems on the quilt sandwich, you won't have to pull the stitches out. Make the necessary adjustments on the machine, then stitch a bit more on the test sandwich until the quilting stitches are nicely formed. Then start quilting for real on the quilt.

Changing threads—different fiber content or even different thread brands—can warrant a thread tension adjustment. You may find that your sewing machine prefers thread that is a certain brand or fiber content. Once you find that magic pairing of sewing machine and

Relieving Tension

Some tension issues that happen while quilting may be resolved by changing to a straight-stitch needle plate. The straight-stitch needle plate has a small hole to accommodate the needle as it moves in one position, as in a straight stitch. The regular needle plate has a slot instead of a single hole to accommodate the needle as it changes position to make various decorative stitches, such as zigzags or buttonholes.

As the needle passes through the fabric, it drags the fabric with it, ever so slightly, as it moves up and down. By switching needle plates, the drag may be reduced just enough to correct minor tension issues. It's worth a try for nagging tension concerns. Just remember to change the plate back again to use any of the decorative stitches, or, rest assured, needles—more specifically, broken needle parts— will fly.

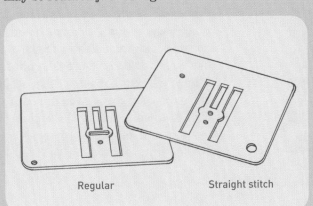

Regular   Straight stitch

thread, stick with it—especially if the machine has a history of being a bit fussy. You may need to experiment a little to find the magic combo. More information about thread will be discussed on pp. 29–31.

IF AT FIRST YOU DON'T SUCCEED . . .TRY AGAIN!

If the stitches simply aren't forming properly, try rethreading the machine, both top and bobbin thread, from start to finish. It's just that simple!

One of the first clues that there is a problem with the upper thread positioning is the presence of a "nest" of thread—excessive tangles of thread—on the bottom of the stitching. The stitches look perfectly fine on top as you sew, then when you look to see what's happening on the underside of the fabric, you gasp a bit and swallow hard when you discover the mess of tangled threads hiding there!

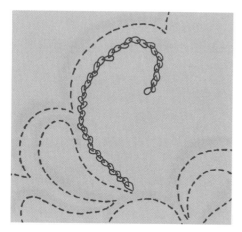

A tangle of threads on the bottom of the quilt means upper thread tension needs an adjustment.

Thread issues on the *bottom* of your work = issues with the *upper* thread path. And you would think just the opposite is true—that thread issues on the bottom of the work mean that something is wrong in the bobbin area of the machine.

Snip the upper thread near the thread spool, release the tension by lifting the presser foot, and pull the thread out through the needle. Always pull thread out of the machine the way it typically works through the machine. Rethread the machine again, carefully following the diagrams on the machine or in the manual.

If you've checked the upper thread path and everything seems to be in its proper place, it's really easy, and very common, to insert the bobbin backward, and even though it seems like that shouldn't make a difference, it does.

Once you rethread the top and bobbin threads along the correct path, you could very well be back to smooth sailing. Clicking your heels together and making a wish might help, too, but only if you are wearing your ruby slippers.

Getting to Know You

My travel sewing machine is a little fussy when it comes to threading the needle. For this machine, I typically thread the needle as usual, following all the proper paths and diagrams on the machine. Then I place my finger near the spool at the very beginning of the thread path and hold the thread firmly. With my other hand, I give a very gentle tug on the thread right at the needle. When I do this, I can feel the thread slide into place between the tension disks, right where it should be. If I forget to take this little extra step and start stitching, my stitches look just fine on top, but there's a storm brewing on the bobbin side of the fabric.

ASK THE EXPERTS

Once you are familiar with your machine, when something isn't right, it only takes a few stitches to recognize it. The sounds aren't the same. The stitches seem labored or stressed. Stop. Take a gander at the sewing machine manual or check the manufacturer's website. If you can't resolve the problem, a visit with your friendly sewing machine dealer may be just the ticket.

AN ANNUAL CHECKUP

The bottom line: Any sewing machine can misbehave. When this happens, stay calm, take a deep breath, and step away, just for a moment. If routine adjustments don't help, contact your dealer for advice. Schedule regular service based on how much you use your machine. At the very least, an annual maintenance appointment will keep all the settings calibrated to perfection.

Pressing Matters

When it comes to quilting and irons, find an iron that is hot, clean, and just a little bit steamy (but only when you really need it), a lot like a good romance novel. By the way, quilters "press," they don't "iron."

You don't have to spend a lot of money to get the job done. A checklist of quilty iron features and why they matter is on p. 12.

A word about the board: A sturdy ironing board with a plain cover is nice, but a "big board"—an ironing board that has a firm, oversize surface—is amazing. The top of the board allows tons more fabric real estate to be pressed at one time. Big boards are typically about 22 in. by 60 in. Your local quilt shop offers ironing board covers that are the perfect size, too.

Maintenance

Tom West is a Swiss-trained sewing machine technician and has taken good care of several of my sewing machines. Here he shares his advice on machine maintenance:

"Solving most sewing machine issues almost always boils down to a simple acronym: TNT—Tension, Needle, and Threading. Check the tension, insert a fresh needle, and double-check the thread path (for both the upper and bobbin thread). A simple mistake, like putting the needle in backward or inserting the bobbin in the wrong way, can create problems. For extra points, clean the hook thoroughly. If you can remove the hook, use a wooden toothpick to clean out the lint that accumulates in the race (the runway for the hook).

"Routine maintenance is easy. The real problems arise when someone brings in a machine that hasn't been serviced in 10 to 12 years, particularly if the machine hasn't been used during that time. The lubricants dissipate or harden, turning into a waxy, shellac-type substance that is difficult to remove. Now, it's much more expensive to get the machine up and running again."

KEY IRON FEATURES TO HAVE

Hot	A hot iron is key when pressing seam allowances.
Heavy	Some heft will make pressing freshly washed yardage a breeze.
Steamy	A steam function is useful for pressing seams and activating fusible glue on interfacing products.
No Leaks	A quality iron shouldn't leak during use. Check your manufacturer's instructions for proper care (some irons prefer distilled water, and some prefer tap).
Energy-saving shut-off	An iron without an automatic shut-off timer can waste energy and cause damage or harm.

 ## Running on Empty

Have you ever been at a social sewing situation and someone raises a fuss, all of a sudden, out of nowhere? The fuss-monkey is easy to find. She (or he) is the one with the monster stack of pieced blocks piled high right behind her sewing machine. She's been happily chain-piecing for the last hour or so, and she's having a miniature meltdown while digging through the stack to see exactly *when* she ran out of bobbin thread.

If your machine doesn't have an alarm announcing that the bobbin is out of thread, be wary of those long piecing runs! If not, you could be the next fuss-monkey! Want a banana?

The "Spit Test"

As a little kid, I loved to watch my mom iron clothes. Maybe it was the steady rhythm of the movements. Or the fragrant smell of clean laundry, fresh from the line. Or maybe it was the spit test. To test when the iron was hot, my mom would lick the end of her finger and barely touch it to the soleplate of the iron. If you heard the *tssst* sound, the iron was ready and the dance could begin. I loved that sound!

These days, I still use the spit test sometimes to see if the iron is hot. More often, the iron beeps to tell me it's ready. Another option that will keep the skin attached to the end of your finger: Take the iron for a little test drive. Swipe the iron, soleplate down, on the ironing board, then place your hand on the swiped area. If the board is hot, the iron is ready.

TIP: Full-size irons draw lots of power. If you find that a relaxed day of sewing causes isolated power outages in your home, it might be the iron. Try moving the iron to another outlet that draws energy from a different circuit. If you are hosting a quilt-a-thon with friends, place irons strategically or reduce the number of irons in use to avoid popping circuit breakers.

Other Handy Tools for Machine Quilting

MACHINE NEEDLES

Sewing machine needle sizes are identified by two numbers—American (size 8 to 19) and European (60 to 120). Typically, both numbers appear on a package of sewing machine needles. The order of the number doesn't affect the size of the needle; for example, an 80/12 is the same as a 12/80. The smaller the number, the finer the needle and the smaller the eye, and a larger number equals a larger needle. The type of fabric and the kind of sewing you do will determine the needle that is best for the job. Quilters typically use needles in the 70/10 to 90/14 range.

Besides the size, needles have different points. Since quilting is typically done with woven fabrics, a universal needle is a fairly standard choice for quilt construction. Jeans needles have a heavier shaft and a sharper point. Sharps are, well, sharper, and make it easier to sew through nonwoven fibers like interfacing. Metallic needles are especially nice for specialty threads used for embellishment because the eye is larger and may keep the threads from breaking and fraying.

PINS

Fabric stretches as it interacts with the presser foot, feed dogs, sewing machine needle, and other fabric. Pins placed strategically along the to-be-sewn seam can reduce or eliminate misbehaving fabric. Pins are like having an extra hand in a tight spot.

Pins are great for piecing, and they also come in handy to secure appliqué shapes before they are sewn. For hand appliqué, a shorter appliqué pin will be less apt to tangle with the thread as the shape is stitched to the background fabric. Larger pins may be used to secure machine-appliqué pieces. Remember: Plastic melts. If you use an appliqué method that involves a hot iron to activate fusible web or fusible interfacing, choose glass-head or heat-resistant pins that won't disintegrate when they come into contact with hot stuff.

Use a heftier pin to secure extra-bulky seams through multiple layers. For example, I use larger pins with a thicker shaft to secure binding strips to the quilt top before machine stitching in place.

And yes, I really do pin my binding to the quilt before sewing. It helps to keep the edge of the quilt flat if I plan the binding placement before I start sewing. Hey, I made it this far in the quilt construction; I want the last few steps to show off my work, not show it up.

 ## Dull, Dull, Dull

Insert a fresh rotary blade in the cutter, and take the first slice of fabric. Heaven! To a quilter, there is nothing like it, often followed by the exclamation, "Why did I wait so long to change that blade?" With every cut, the rotary blade loses just a bit of its sharpness. How do you know when it's time to change the blade?

- When it takes more downward pressure than forward pressure to make a really good, fresh cut.
- Pull the ruler away, and you notice four or five spots along the cut where the fabric is hanging on to its parent desperately by only a thread or two.
- The fabric is fraying a lot more than usual along the freshly cut edge, and you blame the fabric, because it couldn't possibly be the rotary blade.
- The self-healing cutting mat has a noticeable line of tiny threads and fuzz sticking out along a straight line on the mat that, coincidentally, follows the exact same path as the last fabric cut.

Your Cutting Companions

If you're going to use a rotary cutter, then you need to use a self-healing cutting mat and an acrylic ruler. Here are some things to keep in mind when making your purchases:

- Choose a cutting mat as large as your craft space can accommodate. Smaller cutting mats make better traveling companions.
- Keep the cutting mat out of extreme heat. Store it flat for transport. Cutting mats left in a hot car, for example, are likely to bend beyond repair.
- Choose a ruler with clear markings for each quarter inch, half inch, and whole inch at the minimum.
- Acrylic rulers that are laser printed are best. Molded-plastic rulers are softer, are not accurate, and wear down with every cut.
- If you must choose only one ruler, a ruler that is 6½ in. by 12½ in. is ideal. However, a ruler that is about 4 in. by 12 in. may get the most use on my cutting counter because it's easy to handle and convenient for cutting strips. Complete a winning ruler trifecta with a 6-in. square ruler that has a clear bias or diagonal line.
- Specialty rulers and trimming tools add convenience and accuracy—and fun—to specialized cuts.

ROTARY CUTTER

The rotary cutter has a deadly sharp circular blade that cuts through anything with ease. Before the rotary cutter came on the scene, quilters traced templates onto cardboard and cut the fabric around the drawn lines, one piece at a time. The rotary cutter changed everything. The sharp circular blade is attached to the handle at the center of the blade; roll it along the side of a ruler, and it'll cut anything in its path (including fingertips if one isn't careful).

These days, rotary cutters commonly come in three blade sizes for quilting, measured by the diameter in millimeters—60 mm, 45 mm, and 15 mm. The smaller blade is great for maneuvering tight spaces like curved cuts; the larger blade is great for longer cuts. The middle size goes well with everything in between.

TIP: In a pinch, regain a few more decent cuts with a dull blade by cutting through aluminum foil several times.

WHAT THE HECK IS THIS?
GADGETS 101

Specialty rulers, trimming tools, marking pens and pencils, guides, stilettos, fusible stabilizers—you name it! Quilters love gadgets!

There's something for everyone, it seems: a million and one gadgets, each with its specific job, and more being conceived, produced, and sold every day. But is every single gadget the best thing since sliced bread? Maybe. Or maybe not.

We've all been there. You see a new gadget, you watch the demo, and you are inclined to buy. But before you pull out your wallet, ask yourself these questions about your sewing habits:

- Does the gadget replace a technique I use often?

- Does the gadget really make the task easier, better, or more efficient?

- Can I understand how to use the gadget without scratching my head in frustration later? In other words, is it intuitive to use?

- Is it worth the price?

- Does it come with instructions, or are instructions easily available online?

Reserve some space on a sewing-room shelf just for gadget instructions. Many rulers and sewing notions come with written instructions. When you purchase a new tool, and the demonstration is fresh in your mind, you may not need the instructions right away, but give it a few months, a few years, or several projects in between uses, and the instructions may not be so memorable.

SEAM RIPPER

At some point in your quilting career, you'll have to rip out a seam. It happens to the best of us!

Using a seam ripper with a fine, sharp point, hold the fabric in one hand with the seam exposed. It doesn't matter if it's the top or the bottom of the seam. Slide the seam ripper flush with the fabric and insert it in a stitch until the seam ripper cuts the stitch. Repeat every two to three stitches until the entire seam is broken.

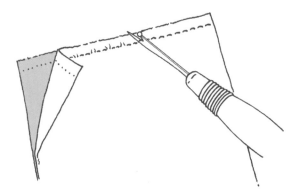

Then gently pull the two fabric layers apart on one end to get it started. Once the seam starts coming apart, keep pulling the fabrics apart and the seam will break apart easily. You'll have lots of little thread-shreds that will brush off the former seam easily. Or you can take the "mom" approach: Once the seam has been severed, hold the two pieces of fabric firmly and pull apart with one swift motion—the same way your mom used to remove a Band-Aid®.

HAND-SEWING NEEDLES: A QUICK REFERENCE

Sharps	Used for securing appliqué, thread basting, securing binding
Betweens	A shorter needle than sharps, used to quilt through multiple layers
Embroidery needle	A long, sharp needle with a larger, flatter eye to accommodate multiple strands of embroidery thread or pearl cotton
Tapestry needle	A long needle with a large eye and a blunt point, used for stitching on mesh fabrics
Crewel needle	A long, sharp needle with an even longer eye for heavier threads or wool work

A Seam Ripper to the Rescue!

Peggy makes such good use of her seam ripper that she has purchased four in the last three years! On one particular occasion, she went to piece the backing for a quilt. Everything was measured, trimmed, and ready to sew. So off she went. She completed the seam connecting the two backing pieces, then opened it up to examine her work and press the result. She discovered that she had sewn the width of one fabric to the length of another! And she was using a directional print. A seam ripper to the rescue!

Step Away from the Sewing Machine: Hand Quilter's Basket

Don't get me wrong; I absolutely love every aspect of making quilts with my sewing machine, but when I really want to relax, handwork—piecing, quilting, embroidery, appliqué—is my go-to technique.

And it's portable. A basket of quilty goodies is always ready to hit the road. Waiting for ballet or sports practice to end, sitting for an extra moment or two at the dentist's or doctor's office, riding in the passenger seat on a road trip, or relaxing on the front porch on a sunny summer's day with a tall glass of lemonade—these are the moments a hand quilter cherishes!

The hand quilter's basket can be a treasure chest for creative fun. From needles to thimbles to quilting frames and more, here's a rundown of all the things that may be needed to bring a quilt from project to treasure.

Here Today, Gone Tomorrow

A few years ago, I absolutely fell in love with a pattern for an embroidered bell pull. It had 12 sections, and each section represented different characters from the song *The Twelve Days of Christmas* in extreme detail. At the time, I had recently purchased a new type of marking pen, and I used it to trace each section of the embroidery. Pipers, dancing ladies, drummers, you name it—not just *one* lady dancing, but all *nine* ladies dancing, each in a different pose arranged across a 6-in.-wide section of the bell pull. In total, the bell pull was 30 in. long.

I traced every single one of those characters onto the cloth. For some reason, even though I was ready to start stitching, I lost interest in the project, rolled up the long, narrow fabric strip neatly, and put it on the shelf for a later date.

I pulled out the prepared fabric a few months later, motivated to start stitching. I unrolled the fabric only to discover that the fabric marking tool I used to make all those detailed markings had faded! Maybe *faded* isn't quite the right word. The marks disappeared. I thought I was seeing things (or not seeing them)! Needless to say, this was not a happy discovery.

Fortunately, when I held the fabric just right, I could *barely* make out the drawings. I managed to recapture most of the lines, with a fair amount of retracing from the original pattern. Do you know, as of this writing, that project remains unfinished? Not a single stitch.

Next time I use a new fabric-marking tool, I'm going to make sure that the time that it takes the marks to fade is *more than* the amount of time it takes to complete the stitching.

HAND-SEWING NEEDLES

Hand sewing brings in a whole different world of sharp points. Hand-sewing needles are sized by number: the larger the number, the finer the needle—that seems counterintuitive, doesn't it? And it's completely the opposite of sewing machine needle sizes. Match thread size to the needle's eye to avoid shredding the thread as it is passed through the fabric.

The eye is punched from one side, so if you have difficulty threading a needle, flip the needle around and try threading it from the other side. Always thread a needle as the thread comes off the spool; don't snip the thread and thread the needle from the thread-end closest to the spool. No spitting on the thread, either. The moisture from the thread left behind on the needle eye can cause the metal to degrade, damaging and shredding the thread.

MARKING TOOLS

Be sure to test any marking tools before you use them on your stitchery. Some may leave unexpected, and unappealing, stains or residue.

- Heat-erasable marking tools: Draw lines, sew, then touch with a hot iron or hot steam, and the marks disappear.

- Air-erasable marking tools: Once marked, the lines disappear in a couple of days.

- Water-erasable marking tools: enough said.

- ¼-in. tape: adhesive, similar to masking tape.

- Hera marker (leaves a depression on the fabric, instead of ink).

FREEZER PAPER

Regular grocery-store-variety freezer paper. Plastic-coated on one side, paper on the other. This stuff is excellent for marking designs, stabilizing fabric, and creating appliqué shapes.

THIMBLE

Thimbles can range from an inexpensive leather thimble to molded metal and jewels, sized to fit your fingertip. I particularly like those that leave a space for your fingernail. As you select a thimble, it should feel comfortable on the end of your middle finger on your dominant hand—not too tight and not too loose! The best thimble is one that is so comfortable that you forget you're wearing it.

SNIPS, OR THREAD SCISSORS

Personally, I'm addicted to these. Cute little cranes with scissor beaks, enameled dots and flowers, funky shapes that look like medieval torture tools, snips with bling-covered lanyards. I have a complete, and ever-growing, collection. Even so, why is it that I sometimes can't find a pair of scissors when I need to cut a thread?

HOOPS

The type and size of hoop you need varies depending on the kind of stitching you're doing. The hoop holds the fabric so hand embroidery or quilting stitches are easier to make, avoiding puckers or pleats in the fabric. Smaller hoops (4 in. to 8 in. across) are perfect for embroidery; larger hoops (10 in. to 12 in. or larger) for hand quilting.

QUILTING FRAME

Okay, so this won't fit in the sewing basket. But it can be a great way to support the weight of a quilt for hand quilting.

Left-Handed Quilters Are Quilters, Too!

It's a right-handed world, even in the sewing room. Sewing tables, scissors, even the sewing machine are oriented around the convenience of a right-handed stitcher.

Left-handed quilters should not despair. Choose tools that are ambidextrous. Look for rulers with clear markings at the top and the bottom of the ruler. Most rotary cutters can and should be reversed so the circular cutter can be on the right side of the handle for easy, accurate, and safe use.

Seek out tools with instructions that accommodate both left- and right-handed illustrations.

Righties will cut from the left edge of the fabric yardage, along the right edge of the ruler or tool, then move the tool to the right, and continue cutting off the left edge of the fabric. Lefties cut fabric from right to left. When watching workshop demonstrations, lefties might get a better perspective by standing opposite the instructor, especially if he or she is right-handed.

Software

When it comes to quilting, the software can be just as important as the hardware. No, I'm not talking about computers. I'm talking about what quilts are made of—fabric!

Fabric 101

Ah-h-h, fabric. It's the stuff that quilts are made of. Shop online or shop in person. What's new, what's new to you, and, especially, what floats your boat? What grabs you? Anything goes! It's your quilt, after all. Some quilters have a knack with color and fabric selection. Others might like a few tips as very special fabrics are selected for a very special quilt project.

Quality Control

All fabric starts out as greige goods—fabric in the raw state—which are printed and rolled, then bolted for sale. It's important to use the best-quality fabric for quilting, and, for the most part, that translates to the best greige goods. The quality of the greige goods boils down to two factors: the fibers used and the density of those fibers. The longer the cotton staple used in the weft and the weave of the fabric, and the higher the thread count—or density—of those fibers in the weave, the better the fabric quality. Why does it matter? Cotton is cotton, right?

It stands to reason that the longer the fibers and the more twists in the thread in the weave, the stronger the fabric, which translates to improved wear and color retention. It can take several weeks or several years to make a single quilt. Doesn't it make sense to use the best-quality fabrics you can afford so the quilt lasts long and holds its color?

How can you tell the quality of quilting fabric? Lesser greige goods will feel a little bit rougher in your hands, and the print may appear a little grainier. The fabric itself is more transparent. Fabrics made from better greige goods will have a smooth, almost silky feel, before and after washing. The printing will be crisp and the colors intense.

Leading and Supporting Roles

When choosing fabric, it's not uncommon, and it is often a good idea, to start with a focus print. Some call it the inspiration fabric—a print, frequently a colorful large-scale print, that sets the theme for the quilt and the secondary fabric selections. The inspiration fabric is typically used as a border, but it doesn't have to be. Some think of the fabric selections for a quilt as if they are actors in a play. Put yourself in the director's chair, and start with the star of the show, or the "main player" fabric, then choose the supporting players—but look out for the villain.

The Quilt's Harmony

Beware of selecting too many main players, which might clash within the overall design. Also, be on the lookout for showoffs. Bright whites in an earthy-themed quilt, for example, can create distracting "holes" that draw the eye away from the action. Similarly, a single dark or brighter-than-bright fabric can throw things off. The colors should build toward a harmonious blend—but every quilt is different, and your quilt's harmony could be acid rock as much as it could be a soothing lullaby.

The supporting actors can be coordinates from the same fabric group, but my preference is to mix it up a bit and select textures and solids that support the quilt's theme and overall aesthetic. Examine the main player fabric; look for colors that could be used as secondary players or accents, then go on a treasure hunt in your stash or in the shop. Sometimes the main player doesn't reveal itself until some of the blocks are assembled.

Value plays a role, too, and by *value* I mean dark and light. *Dark* isn't always dark—a medium fabric may become the dark player in a soft, blended quilt. Choose a combination of light- and dark-value fabrics, unless you're going for a more blended look.

Making a test block or two is always a good idea. Put the test blocks on a design wall or throw a piece of scrap batting over an open door, then place the blocks on it. Stand back, evaluate your color and value choices, then adjust as needed. It's better to decide a change is in order after making a few blocks than after making a whole stack of them.

 ## Better Late Than Never

Karen signed up for quilt camp: three days of quilty indulgence, working on just one project. She received her supply list and went in search of the perfect fabrics. The pattern called for a bold stripe for a pieced sashing element, plus scraps, selected with the stripe as the inspiration. She found a stripe, then she chose the scrappy fabrics for the rest of the quilt. Karen just loved the scrappy fabrics. The stripe was nice, but she wasn't necessarily in love.

At the retreat, Karen assembled the scrappy blocks and made the pieced sashing elements, then assembled the quilt center. But something was wrong, and Karen wasn't sure what. That stripe didn't seem to work as well as she wanted it to. Ignoring the inner voice telling her something wasn't right, she set off to the quilt shop to audition prospective border prints to complete the quilt. And, indeed, there it was, the perfect border fabric to complete the project. Excellent!

But wait! What's this over here? Another striped fabric that matched the scraps and the border perfectly. Only one more evening of sewing was left during the retreat. Karen purchased the stripe and the border print and headed back to the retreat so she could remove all the unloved striped fabric and replace it with the new stripe. This was no small feat, as replacing the stripe made the project much more complicated.

By the end of the weekend, Karen's quilt was complete. Sometimes it's worth the trouble to change direction, even late in the game. When you know it's right, it's right, and that's all there is to it!

Goldilocks and the Three Fabrics

You're in line at the fabric shop. How do you make sure that you purchase not too little, not too much, but just the right amount of fabric to complete the project?

Of course, whenever possible, refer to the pattern. Yardage requirements are nearly always clearly displayed on the back of a pattern or on the first page of the pattern instructions, but if you are making changes to the size of the quilt or if you don't have the pattern with you, a little math may be required.

For starters, when purchasing fabric by the yard, count on 40 in. of usable fabric width as it comes off the bolt. When you start cutting, expect a little waste at the fabric selvage edges and in between strip slices. Even though the selvage-to-selvage measurement might be greater, for computation purposes, consider 36 in. (1 yd.) of fabric to be closer to 35 in. by 40 in. in usable fabric area.

It's dangerous to generalize, but if you start with the math, come up with a number on the fly, and want a fast reality check, these estimates may help you stay in range at the cutting counter.

- Borders with no piecing typically require a range of 1 yd. to 2 yd., depending on the size of the quilt and the width of the border. Plan for at least seven to eight width-of-fabric strips, and multiply the estimated number of strips by the border width.

- Double-fold binding is usually in the ½ yd. to ⅔ yd. range. Measure the perimeter of the quilt, divide by 40 in. to calculate the number of strips needed, then multiply by the width you like to cut the binding. For me, that's 2¼ in. Then divide by 36 in. That's how many yards to get.

Quick Tips for Choosing Fabric Colors

- A little bit of yellow can go a long way.
- Red typically registers as dark value.
- Brights typically register as medium value.
- *Dark* and *light* are relative terms, based on the other values present.
- You can't have too much green. Many fabric prints are floral themed. In nature, flowers have stems and leaves, green ones. A decent stash of green can be a gold mine for accents and bindings!

- Background fabric gets a bit tricky. The background can be the largest quantity of any one fabric needed for a quilt top. Do a bit of math; if the quantity for a large lap- to queen-size quilt falls in the 1½-yd. to 3-yd. neighborhood, you're likely in the ballpark.

- Generally, when a quilt has lots of piecing, you'll need more fabric. Sometimes lots more. All those little seams hidden on the inside of the quilt can add up.

If you really, really love your fabric choices, and don't want to risk making substitutes, start in on the project right away. Fabric prints have a relatively short lifespan on the store shelf. Popular prints can disappear at lightning speed. Once you begin cutting for the project, you can usually tell, fairly quickly, if the quantity you purchased is going to be adequate to finish the deed.

Should you find yourself in a shortage situation and the fabric has disappeared off the shelf at the local shop, or if you procured your fabric possession while away from your usual fabric purchase haunts, you may still be in luck with an online search. Be prepared to pay a little extra on the yardage in addition to shipping costs. If you are *really* lucky, you might get the errant fabric on sale.

When all else fails, your quilty friends may have *your* fabric tucked away in *their* stash. Imagine that! Prepare yourself for some creative negotiations.

40/80/120

When it comes to backing quantity, it's all about 40 in. and multiples of 40 in. Each multiple of 40 represents one 40-in.-wide selvage-to-selvage fabric strip; 80 in. is two 40-in.-wide strips, and 120 in. is three.

Start with the size of the quilt top. Add an extra 6 in. to 12 in. to each dimension, and that's the area of your backing fabric. So, if the quilt top is 50 in. by 70 in., the backing needs to be at least 56 in. by 76 in. For the most efficient use of backing fabric, consider each dimension of the quilt (56 in. or 76 in. in our example), and choose the dimension that is closest to, but not over, 40 in. (or a multiple of 40 in.).

Then multiply the number in the remaining dimension by 1, 2, or 3 (corresponding to 40/80/120). Have I lost you yet? Then divide by 36 in. to calculate the number of yards needed for the backing.

The desired backing area of our example is 56 in. by 76 in. The second dimension—76 in.—

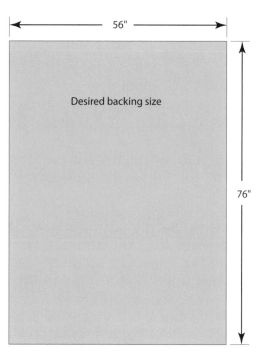

To calculate yardage needed for the backing, start by adding 6 in. to the quilt top dimensions.

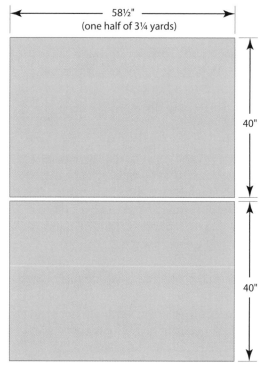

Fabric is sold by the yard, not the inch. Round up to the nearest quarter, half, or third yard for backing quantity.

is closest to 80 in. without going over. So, two 40-in.-wide fabric strips are needed. Two multiplied by 56 in. is 112 in. That's how many inches of fabric to buy, but fabric is sold by the yard (at least in the United States), so divide 112 by 36 for a total of 3.1 yd. Round up to 3¼ yd. or more because fabric is sold by quarters, halves, and thirds of a yard rather than tenths.

Other backing fabric considerations include the following:

- Some longarm quilters like extra backing fabric, so if you're sending the quilt to a longarm quilter, check first before settling on a fabric amount.

- When considering directional fabrics for the quilt backing, calculate the yardage needed based on the orientation of the print.

- A row of pieced blocks or scraps from the quilt top sewn between the backing panels can supplement the yardage. Instead of three

Go Big or Go Home!

When I speak to quilter groups, I'm often asked how much fabric I buy if I see some fabric in a shop that I like, but for which I don't necessarily have a project in mind. I run though the checklist on p. 26 and purchase accordingly.

widths of backing fabric, two widths and a strategically placed row of scrap blocks sewn in between the two fabric widths can save money and make nice use of leftovers.

Of course, most quilt shops stock a variety of extra-wide backing fabrics (90 in. to 110 in. wide). No math, no guessing, no piecing involved.

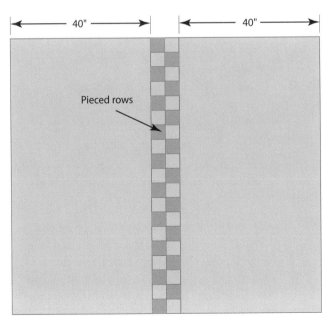

Add a pieced strip between backing strips to make efficient use of fabric leftovers.

FABRIC AMOUNTS CHEAT SHEET

Does it have potential as a focus or main player print?	2–3 yd.
Is it a good backing prospect?	5 yd. at least, maybe more
White-on-white or cream-on-cream prints	3 yd.
Green	1–2 yd.
Purple (my favorite color)	How much is left on the bolt?

 ## Whoops!

Peggy found a pattern that would make a perfect patriotic-themed quilt. The pattern featured log cabin blocks that, when arranged a certain way, formed a large star. Using a photograph as a guide, Peggy loaded her fabric color choices into computer software that would calculate fabric yardage for the quilt in the size she wanted. Using the fabric calculations, Peggy found exactly what she needed in her stash and started cutting.

In one of those heart-stopping instants, halfway through the cutting, Peggy realized that she forgot to adjust the block size from the program default. She was cutting strips for 6-in. blocks, but she really wanted to make 9-in. blocks to finish the quilt faster. Since she already had half of the fabrics cut, she kept going.

The quilt turned out beautifully, made of a whopping 100 blocks instead of about half that many, as originally intended.

Size Issues

When upsizing or downsizing a quilt pattern, adding more blocks or reducing the number of blocks can impact fabric needs for other elements of the quilt as well. Don't forget to consider borders, sashing and cornerstone elements, binding, and backing.

Design elements may be driven by an odd or even number of blocks, so by simply adding a row of blocks, the pattern may be thrown off a bit. Increasing or decreasing in multiples of two blocks may be necessary to maintain quilty harmony.

Whodunnit?

The first time I made a "mystery" quilt, I was very new to this whole quilty business. Every month, the local quilt shop provided a new clue to solve the mystery, which involved cutting and assembling various parts of the quilt until the whole project was revealed in the last step.

The first step of a mystery involves selecting fabric for the entire project. Choosing fabric for a quilt can be difficult when you know what the pattern looks like; choosing it for an unknown pattern is a puzzle all by itself.

For my first mystery quilt, only three fabrics were needed: a focus print and two coordinates. It was revealed that the focus print would also become the border, but some of the focus print was needed for the quilt center, too.

For my mystery focus fabric, I chose a fun blue-and-white print with cute chickens tossed all over. For the remaining two prints, I chose two solid-reading accent colors—yellow and red. Both were really bright.

The smallest quantity needed for the quilt was the focus print, my favorite of the three selections. The remaining two fabric quantities—the yellow and red—were twice or three times the quantity of the focus print. Hmm.

As I assembled the quilt, I was concerned that I really wasn't using very much of the blue that I liked so much. Sure enough, the final quilt was really more of a red and yellow quilt than anything blue. I decided that the next time I did a mystery project, I would choose my favorite prints and colors based on quantity. Still, that mystery quilt is one of my favorites. But it's very yellow.

Flannel & Friends

A common fabric choice for a cozy quilt is flannel. Flannel tends to stretch a bit more than flat cotton. That can be a double-edged sword. Stretchier fabrics can be forgiving when matching seams, but flannel isn't necessarily the best choice for a quilt with lots of little pieces; flannel likes big spaces.

What about silk, rayon, wool, poly plush? Are any fabrics off limits? Not really. Perhaps the most common quilting fabric is quilting cotton.

It's predictable. But any fabric can be turned into a quilt. Special care may be required as different fabrics are sewn next to each other. Really stretchy fabrics, like T-shirts, may need to be stabilized with interfacing before they are sewn next to quilting cottons that don't stretch as much.

Weave, Weft, Woof!

Did you ever notice when sewing two pieces of fabric together—just fabric, no pieced elements involved—that one gets longer than the other by the time you are done sewing the two pieces together? Maybe it's because of the fabric weave.

Quilting cotton fabrics are woven. The warp (the lengthwise grain) is the least stretchy part of the fabric. The weft (the width of fabric) is stretchier than the warp. And the bias, the imaginary diagonal line that crosses warp and weft at a 45-degree angle, is super-stretchy.

Take any piece of woven fabric that has been cut with the fabric grain, and you can actually see the difference in stretch even when the selvage isn't present. Gently pull outward along the straight of grain. One side will give a little, and another will hardly give at all. A similar tug from corner to corner will reveal lots of give in the fabric.

Since you may not be able to tell stretchiness at a glance, and since it's very possible to sew a stretchy edge against another, creating the potential for one of the two fabrics to "grow" while sewing them, extra pins can add control.

Whenever possible, to keep stretchiness to a minimum, especially around the outside edges of the quilt, cut fabric strips for borders and sashing strips along the lengthwise grain.

To Wash or Not to Wash? That Is the Question

Confession: I'm a prewasher. As soon as I come home from a fabric acquisition expedition, I put my purchases directly into the wash basin with hot, hot, hot water and a little squirt of dish soap. The hot water helps to preshrink the fabric and removes excess dye, reducing the chance (theoretically) that the dye could run into adjoining fabrics in my quilt. I wash like colors together. The soapy water also removes any chemicals used in the dyeing and finishing process.

I prefer using the basin rather than throwing the fabric directly into the washer because I can see if any of the colors run. If the running dye is excessive, I may evict the offending fabric from my stash, so it's sure not to run in the finished quilt—its ultimate destination.

Once the fabrics have soaked in the hot water about 15 minutes or so, I drain the basin and add cold water to rinse out the soap and cool the fabrics. Then I send the fabrics through the spin cycle in my washing machine to remove excess water and, after that, I dry them on high heat, for maximum shrinkage. Once this is done, I press the fabrics and fold them into quarters for storage or use.

After a quilt is made, I keep it unwashed for as long as possible. Every time a quilt is washed, it loses color, just a little bit. And the quilting adds a bit of pucker to the quilting textures and the piecework—all well and good—but my preference is the look of the freshly quilted stitches before washing.

> **TIP:** Because fabric dyes can run unpredictably, even after they've been prewashed, I rarely wash a quilt without using a dye-catching sheet. When giving a quilt as a gift, I place a dye-catching laundry sheet in a pouch with washing instructions for the quilt, and give it along with the quilt.

Beware of Bleach

Judy made a table runner for her daughter's anniversary, appliquéd with flowers and leaves along the entire length. Judy made each appliqué piece with her very own hand-dyed fabric created during a dyeing workshop a few years earlier. All the fabrics had been treated with dye stabilizer until they passed the "rinse until the water is clear" test.

The finished project was gorgeous, and Judy could hardly wait to give it to her daughter. Just one more rinse to remove any last traces of the markings from the appliqué shapes.

You guessed it, the colors ran: Reds and pinks bled into the white background fabric. Judy contacted the instructor from the dyeing class, who agreed that there was nothing to be done. Judy almost gave the runner to her daughter anyway, but she was determined to make it perfect. However, none of the variety of products that promised to remove the unwanted color bleeds worked.

How about adding a little bleach? Just a little on the white fabric, with the very tip of a cotton swab. What could go wrong?

The white got whiter immediately—then fingers of bleach reached into the appliqué shapes, ruining them. To top it off, the bleach turned the white background yellow. The ruined runner went into the trash.

Judy's advice: Check all hand-dyed fabrics for colorfastness, and even then there's no guarantee. If something does run, live with it. Sometimes continuing to find the perfect fix will only make things worse.

Unraveled: The Basic 411 on Thread

Thread: It might be the most easily overlooked element in a quilt, often purchased as an afterthought. And yet, thread is what holds it all together. The majority of thread in my quilting cabinet is cotton, for one reason: I use cotton fabrics in the quilts I make, and cotton thread will age at the same rate as the fabric used for the project.

Thread is packaged by the size of the thread, often designated by two numbers separated by a slash. The first number stands for the weight of the fiber. The finer the fiber, the higher the number. The second number is the number of strands.

All kinds of bad things are avoided when you use the highest-quality thread you can afford. This is so important, that you should go back and read that last sentence again. Let's consider why. Thread is made by twisting together strands of cotton, or *staple*. The longer

BEYOND COTTON: OTHER THREAD FIBERS AND THEIR USES

Coated long-staple cottons	For hand quilting. Don't use these in the sewing machine.
Rayon	A fiber derived from cellulose. Typically intense color. Adds sheen to quilting.
Polyester	For quilting or piecing. Often used in the bobbin for piecing. Excellent for machine embroidery.
Metallic	For embellishment.
Silk	Very fine. Favored for hand appliqué. Over time, silk threads may stretch and loosen.
Wool	Heavier. Creates bold lines, often used to secure wool appliqué by hand.
Nylon, monofilament	Can be stretchy. Used for machine quilting or to secure appliqué where no specific color thread is desired.

 ## Old Spools?

Let's say you just inherited your Aunt Millie's sewing basket. You discover lots of really cool vintage gadgets, including some of her very old thread on cute wooden spools. My advice: Use the thread as a decoration in the curio cabinet. Using old thread is like having mystery meat for dinner: You really don't know the fiber content, or the quality of that fiber content. Cotton thread ages, so it's likely to shred and break easily. And that wooden spool may not pass the test of time, either. Splinters and burrs on the spool itself may create more trouble than it's worth.

the staple, the fewer fuzzy, cottony ends stick out and break off to become lint. That means that as you sew like a maniac, lint won't accumulate as quickly in all the nooks and crannies of the sewing machine. It stands to reason that higher-quality threads cost more—but they cost less, in the long run, in terms of sewing machine maintenance. Using higher-quality thread is like taking out an insurance policy or an extended warranty on your sewing machine.

Shorter-staple cottons can be masked to look like longer-staple cotton with coating. So with that same level of insane sewing, the coating wears off as the shorter-staple cotton is fed through the sewing machine at a kajillion stitches a minute. Little bits of coating transfer to the machine and accumulate, along with all those extra little fuzzy lint ends, requiring more frequent machine cleaning and potentially damaging buildup.

The second number on the thread spool after the slash identifies the thickness of the thread, as determined by the number of plies. The thickness of the thread may help determine the size needle to use (the more plies, the larger the needle needed to accommodate the thread without breakage).

Batting, the Invisible Ingredient

Walk into a craft store and head to the batting section. It's tucked away in the far corners of the store, and with so many choices, it's easy to see why a batting purchase can be confusing. You don't even see it on your finished quilt, so why does it matter what kind of batting you use in the quilt sandwich?

You've put a fair amount of effort into creating a beautiful quilt top and selecting a coordinating backing, so don't drop the ball when it comes to choosing the batting. Fiber

What Is Scrim?

Most batting is felted. Scrim is like a very soft, lightweight, tiny fabric screen, usually made of polyester that lives in the middle of the batting. The scrim is sandwiched between the batting fibers, then the fibers are needled into the scrim. This helps the batting hold its shape over time, but it can create a less-than-appealing batting for hand quilting because the scrim doesn't separate to make way for needle and thread as easily as natural fibers do.

content options include cotton, polyester, bamboo, wool, silk, and fusibles, and each batting type can impact how you quilt the project—the type of batting you use in your quilt determines how far away your quilting stitches need to be.

Each type of fiber adds different characteristics to the finished quilt as well. Cotton/polyester blend batting usually holds up to more frequent washings, but it isn't as nice for hand quilting, tends to remember long-term folds, and can be weighty. My favorite, 100 percent wool batting, is forgiving with folds and quilts beautifully by hand and machine, but it needs a more delicate washing regimen. Fusible batting can eliminate some of the basting steps, but it requires that you wash the quilt once it's complete to remove

It's All Because of the Batting

Nearly all of the quilt patterns and instructions I write suggest pressing seam allowances to one side when piecing, as opposed to pressing seams open. I like it when seam intersections "nest," reminding me that my piecing accuracy is on track. Also, I tend to do a lot of in-the-ditch quilting (straight-line sewing through all the layers of a quilt sandwich along the seam allowance), and if seams are pressed open, in-the-ditch quilting can sever the seams, compromising the quilt top construction over the long haul. Technically, though, the most convincing reason I know of to press my quilt seams to one side, as opposed to pressing them open, is the batting.

Batting is designed to stay inside fabric that is 60 to 80 threads per inch—think of the thread count on fine sheets. The lower the thread count, the more likely the batting will migrate or "beard" to the exterior of the quilt as the quilt is used and washed and used again.

When you press seams open without increasing the number of stitches sewn per inch, you are creating a sneaky "portal" for the batting to escape from the center of the quilt as the quilt is used.

the fusible chemicals. Stiff fiber content bats may serve well for art pieces and dimensional projects like bags, but they don't work well for functional bed quilts.

Each of your quilted projects may have different characteristics that lend better to one type of batting over another. Like anything else, batting selection can be very much a personal preference.

Choosing a Pattern

Like fabric, patterns can be tempting. Simply owning the pattern can almost be as good as making the project. Having the pattern in your library fulfills the notion that you *could* make the project when all the conditions are right: The

right fabric is procured, the right tools are at hand, and the right rainy-day quilting mood is set.

Most patterns are a relatively small investment in the scheme of quilty things, but buyer's remorse, or worse—frustration—can set in if you choose poorly. Before you buy, ask yourself a few questions:

• Do I love the pattern or just the fabric in the photograph?

• Is there a sample available in the shop where the pattern is for sale so I can take a closer look at the quilt construction?

• Does the project have enough challenge to hold my interest? Will I learn something new?

- Will it accommodate techniques I like?

- Are the illustrations clear and plentiful?

- Do pattern details trail off at the end? Or do the instructions remain strong for the entire pattern?

If you purchase a pattern with the intent to make the project exactly like the one in the picture, you may be disappointed. The life expectancy of the pattern is typically longer than the availability of the fabric used in the cover photograph—the sample for a pattern published in a book might be sewn 18 months before the book's publication. Try to keep an open mind and visualize the shapes and designs in the fabric that made you fall in love with the pattern. Look at the characteristics of the fabrics that appeal to you—large scale, small scale, bold prints, soft colors—and select new fabrics from your stash or from the store that might make good substitutes.

Before making a single cut or sewing the first stitch, read the pattern from start to finish. Get a feel for the techniques used, be aware of the tricky spots in the instructions, and follow the tips and hints in the pattern if they are available.

POWERING THROUGH THOSE SUBPAR PATTERNS

If a pattern isn't quite up to par, all is not lost. Sometimes a few clues and a little bit of math can save the day. First, if you reach a challenging part of the construction, step away, especially when you are tired. Sometimes a fresh perspective turns on all kinds of lightbulbs, and point-of-no-return mistakes can be avoided. Check the publisher or designer website for corrections: It's possible an error was discovered post-publication and the clarity you need is cyber-steps away. Don't let your storage space gain another unfinished object because something in the pattern is missing or because something is easily misunderstood.

Snip, Snip!

Your next quilt is right in front of you—fabric, thread, batting, and the tools. The only thing that stands between you and the sewing machine is that first cut. And the next one. And the one after that. That tiny little voice inside reminds you . . . don't mess it up!

AVOIDING V'S AND W'S

Almost without exception, a quilt begins to be a quilt with a straight-edge cut. One cut leads to another to make strips. The strips are then cross-cut into squares, and rectangles, and triangles, which are sewn together again.

But things can go off course from that very first cut. Cut a strip, open it up, and it's not quite a straight line. Instead, a little point at the fold forms a V-shape, or a W-shape if the fabric was folded twice for the cut. The key to making every strip perfectly straight is to align the fold—both folds, if the fabric is folded in half,

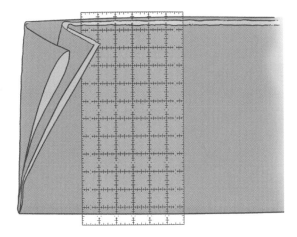

Align horizontal folds in the fabric with horizontal ruler lines.

Anatomy of a Well-Written Pattern

- The finished size of the project, and a full-color photograph of the project on the cover
- Complete yardage requirements, including any special notions required to complete the project, noted on the back cover
- Detailed cutting instructions, illustrations, and labels
- Pressing instructions, including pressing direction symbols in the illustrations as appropriate
- Tips
- Measurements for interim steps, to check progress
- Website information

then in half again—with the horizontal lines on the ruler. Measure the strip while keeping the folds in check with the vertical ruler lines, and V's and W's will lose their points, and the strips will be as straight as an arrow. Check and adjust the fabric after every two or three cuts to keep strips straight.

CUTTING PANELS AND BORDER STRIPES

Preprinted panels can be hard to resist! Add a border to a full-size panel, and the quilt is ready to use in a jiffy. With a few sashing strips and a border, turn a book panel into a quilt that turns naptime into story time. Border stripes add exquisite detail and dress up the perimeter of any quilt.

Here are some tips for working with preprinted panels:

- Accommodate for seam allowances by cutting at least ¼ in. away from any critical printed design element.

- Decorative or repeating stripes used as a border treatment on a quilt are especially nice with mitered corners. Mitered corners on borders can save time when adding multiple borders to a quilt. To get a lot of practice, try making The Miter Touch Quilt on p. 100.

- Avoid washing preprinted panels until after they are sewn and quilted into the quilt. Prewashing could distort or shrink or change the shape of the panel elements. As it is, panels may come off the bolt a bit distorted.

- To straighten an errant panel, spray it lightly with a starch alternative and press it with a hot, steamy iron while the panel is still damp. Hold or pin one side of the panel to the ironing surface and press away from the secured section of the quilt to reshape the panel.

- If the panel is really out of whack, blocking may be the ticket. Dampen the fabric with a light mist of cool water, reshape it with some insistent tugging, and pin each side liberally to a large ironing board or to the floor or carpet (make sure to cover the carpet with plastic first, so that dyes don't transfer). Let the panel dry, undisturbed. This blocking process will be much more successful if family pets are otherwise distracted during the drying process.

DANG-NAB-IT! IT'S CUT WRONG!

Now what? You followed along carefully, measuring twice (or more), and cutting once. But the best-laid plans can be overridden with one errant cut.

If the miscut happens early in the game, it's likely that cutting conservatively will save the day. In fact, it's a really good idea to cut the largest pieces first from the recommended yardage. Then the leftovers from the bigger cuts can be used for the smaller elements. But if the miscut piece can't be made up by cutting a new square (or whatever shape) from the remaining fabric, you have only a few choices.

Clearly, buying more fabric is the easiest solution, but you can substitute from your stash or from the store with a similar but different fabric. Easy enough, unless an exact match is needed.

You can piece fabric leftovers, making smaller scraps bigger. Sew smaller pieces together with a straight seam and press the seam open. No one will notice, particularly with solid colors or busy micro-prints. If the missing fabric is a large-scale print, you might not get away with the repair as easily, unless you take the effort to match the prints. And if you aren't happy with the fix-up results, an appliquéd patch covering the boo-boo could save the day.

 ## My First Encounter with Border Stripes

When I first started quilting, I made quite a few samples for the local quilt shop. Because I made a lot of samples, it was easy for Janet, the shop owner, to assume I knew exactly what she wanted when she gave me a new project.

One time, Janet handed me a kit. I remember vaguely that she said something about a border stripe fabric. And off I went.

A week or two later I returned to the shop, proud to reveal the completed quilt. I don't think I'll ever forget the look on Janet's face at that moment! She expected to see the border stripe cut along the lengthwise grain, forming a solid frame around the quilt. Having never worked with a border stripe before, I cut the strips from selvage to selvage, across the stripes, so that the border looked reminiscent of a barcode. (It looked okay to me!) The moral of the story is: Never assume anything!

MATCHING PRINTS

Matching prints in a seam can be a tricky operation. However, it's especially effective on large-scale prints where the print repeat is easily identified. It's a wonderful way to correct a cutting mistake or seam backing fabric.

Lay the two fabric pieces on top of each other so the fabric edges disappear in the print. Make sure you have enough fabric to re-create the necessary size piece of fabric.

With the fabrics right sides together, stab a pin through the matching design elements, establishing the ¼-seam allowance.

Then, find a few easily identifiable points—like the center of a flower, the point of a bird's beak, the tip of a leaf, or a ripple or bend in a geometric curve.

Use an erasable marking tool to draw a line connecting several of the points on each fabric layer—the same points on each layer—to create matching lines. Carefully cut ¼ in. away from each line, one above and one below the line. Be sure the line isn't cut off on either fabric!

Place the fabrics right sides together with the lines—well—aligned! Stab pins through the points of interest identified earlier—the flower center or leaf points, as it were. Be sure the pin stabs through the same point in both fabrics, and be aware that the prints will look strange. Pin along the line liberally.

To match a spot in the fabric print, stab it with a pin to align that element on both layers of fabric.

Sew ¼ in. away from the raw edge. The seam and both drawn lines should occupy the same space in the universe.

Press the seam open. With a little luck, the seam should disappear in the print! Want to know a secret? One of the panels in The Miter Touch Quilt was pieced this way (p. 100). Can you tell which one?

Let's Make Blocks

A common starting point for constructing a traditional quilt is making the blocks.

Blocks

Most traditional quilts start with an arrangement of quilt blocks. Not squares, *blocks*. And by the way, *quilts* aren't *blankets*. Quilts are stitched together with love. Blankets are, well, blankets.

Back to the blocks. Perhaps the most common block shape is a square. But some blocks aren't square at all—hexagons, equilateral triangles, apple cores, tumblers. Some blocks are made from one piece of fabric; many follow an arrangement of four, nine, sixteen, or more geometric elements.

 ## The ¼-in. Seam

I'm happy to consider Susan K. Cleveland (of PiecesBeWithYou.com) a quilty friend within the universe of quilt designers. If you've ever used any of the quilting tools she has developed, then you know that her ideas and her instructions are meticulous and spot-on. So, when I consider precision piecing and quilting, Susan comes to mind as someone who might be able to offer some outstanding advice. She says:

"Ah, the nasty quarter inch. I have two ideas that help to refine a quilter's seam allowance. First, it's very difficult to sew a straight seam without the benefit of using all of the machine's feed dogs. When the right feed dog isn't completely covered with fabric, it's like driving with one's right wheels in the mud. The fancier a machine is, the more this is an issue because the feed dogs are set wider. There is a remedy, though. Replace the ¼-in. foot with an open-toe foot and simply move the needle over to the right. Now even a ¼-in. seam allowance will cover all feed dogs with fabric and allow the machine to push fabric through much more evenly. A seam guide of some sort is needed to determine where the fabric's edge needs to be for accuracy.

"The second idea is that one seam allowance does not fit all. When we press seam allowances to one side, there is fabric taken up in the *turn of the cloth*. Fabric bends back over the thread and back onto itself, so the thickness of fabric and thread determines the amount of fabric taken in the turn of the cloth. The turn of the cloth must be accounted for in the scant ¼-in. seam allowance. A thicker fabric and thread takes more; thinner ones, less. So, set up your machine the best you can, do a test, and then adjust. Don't be surprised if different fabric/thread combinations require a slightly different seam allowance."

The Perfect ¼-in. Seam, and Why It Matters

If you are going to make a pieced quilt block, the ¼-in. seam is your best friend or your nemesis. New quilters strive to identify it. Experienced quilters seek to master it. Garment sewists tangle with it. There's even a foot for it.

All the math, all the finished/unfinished terminology comes down to mastering this measurement representing one-quarter of the width of a man's thumb.

Quilter's Math— Pieced Blocks

Let's say you want to make an 8-in. block. And you have four pieces of fabric you want to use to make the block—a simple four-patch, two rows of two squares of fabric sewn together.

Two rows of two squares of fabric make a four-patch block.

What size do you cut each of the four fabric pieces? The obvious answer is 4½ in. square. Obvious? Huh?

THE GRID

Let's go back and take a closer look at the problem. First of all, even though it doesn't say it, our finished block will be 8 in. square. *Finished* is the key word. That means that once the block is sewn somewhere in the middle of the quilt, all you'll see is 8 in. of fabric. What you won't see is the ¼ in. of fabric—or the seam allowance—on all four sides of the block. Like the seams on your clothes, it's inside. To calculate the size of the *unfinished* block, take the finished block dimension—8 in.—and add ¼ in. times 2, or ½ in., for 8½ in. square.

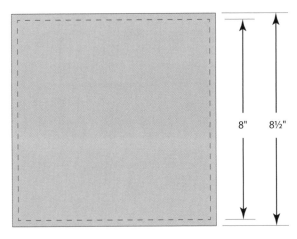

The size of the unfinished block is the finished size of the block plus ½ in.

When doing quilter's math, convert measurements to finished sizes, then switch back to the unfinished size by adding back the ½ in. for cutting. For the simple four-patch example, start with the finished dimension of the block (8 in.) and divide it by 2 (because two rows of two fabric pieces will make up the block construction). The result is 4 in. Then add back ½ in. for the seam allowance. Cut the squares 4½ in. See, I told you it was obvious!

UP THE ANTE: A SAWTOOTH STAR

Let's add some challenge. A sawtooth star is a little more complex, but still fairly basic.

Let's say the finished block size is 12 in. If we break the block into a square grid pattern, we can see that this block fits on a 4×4 grid.

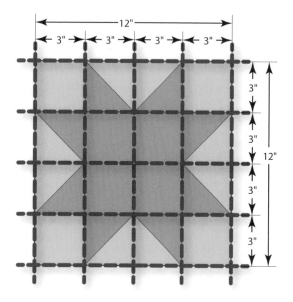

The sawtooth star block can be broken into a 4 × 4 grid pattern.

TIP: Nearly every square traditionally pieced block can be broken down into a grid, a basic 2x2, 3x3, 4x4, etc. Then the grid can be evaluated for its shape complexities.

We can break the block down and see that there is one big center square, four smaller corner squares, and four rectangle sides. Each of the rectangle sides is composed of three triangles—two smaller triangles on two corners and one large center triangle—otherwise known as a flying geese unit. What size should each block element be cut?

Let's start with the easy stuff first—the four corners and the center. The grid breaks the block into 16 squares. Each side of the block is four squares wide. If I divide the finished size of the block by 4, or divide 12 in. by 4, the result is 3. That means each grid unit is 3 in. square. The corner is also the same as one grid section or 3-in. finished size. Add back ½ in. for the seam allowances, and the corner squares are cut 3½ in.

Using the same logic, the center is four grid units, or two across by two down. Two times 3 in. is 6—that's the finished size. Add the seam allowance, and the result is 6½ in., which is the unfinished size and the size to cut the center square.

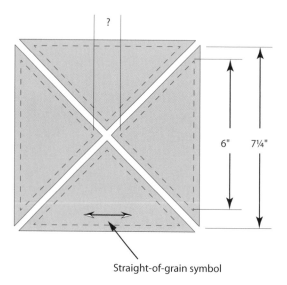

Straight-of-grain symbol

The center of a quarter-square triangle makes converting from finished to unfinished size a little more complicated.

It gets tricky with the flying geese units. A flying geese unit has one quarter-square triangle—that's a square that has been cut in half twice along the diagonal.

The finished size of the quarter-square triangle is 6 in., or two grid units wide along its base. Because of the triangle shape, we can't simply add back the ½-in. seam allowance. The problem isn't the outer corners; the problem is in the center of the square. Once the square is cut, the finished shape will have seam allowances all the way around it. To calculate the point-to-point measurement in the center of the square requires some pretty strange math—great for a high-school geometry problem, but do we really have to go there?

Nope. Rather than do the weird math over and over again, it's easy to use a formula to determine what size to cut the square from which two diagonal cuts will produce four quarter-square triangles. Start with the finished size of the longest side of the triangle—on our diagram, that's two grid units long or 6 in.—then add 1¼ in., which makes 7¼ in. Then cut the square in half twice on the diagonal. The resulting triangles are quarter-square triangles, four triangles from one square. As a not-so-coincidental coincidence, the straight of grain follows the longest side of the triangle, and the bias follows the shorter sides.

A similar mathematical dilemma burps up with the two smaller half-square triangles on the corner of the flying geese units. Fortunately, there's another formula to make life easy. Start with the finished size of one of the short sides of the triangle—in our example, one grid, or 3 in., and add ⅞ in. for a total of 3⅞ in. Then cut the square in half once. The resulting triangles are half-square triangles: two triangles from one square. The straight of grain follows the shorter sides.

Now the block is ready to sew.

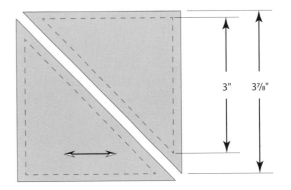

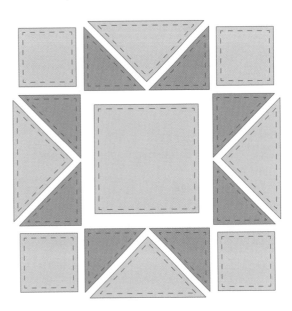

The unfinished block parts look like they'll never fit together, but they will, if your quilter's math is correct.

MORE

Is your brain tired yet? Let's push it a bit more. What if we replace the center of the star with a nine-patch, and put four-patches in the corners?

We already know that the original block center is two grids square, or 6 in. by 6 in. To make a nine-patch that fits in that space, divide the finished size (6 in.) by 3 (for the three units along each side of the nine-patch). This equals 2.

Changing the block elements is easy when you understand quilter's math.

Here's the good news: With so many ways to achieve the same result, quilters have lots of choices. It's nearly impossible to get bored. And it's fun to experiment with different techniques.

TIP: By the way, say what you will about the imperial measurement system, but inches break down nicely into ¼-in. increments, which play out well on most acrylic quilting rulers. Just sayin'! On the flip side, one could argue that all this math is easier in decimals than it is in fractions.

Don't forget to add back ½ in. for the seam allowance. The unfinished or cut size of each square is 2½ in.

The corner is one grid unit, or 3 in. finished size. To make a four-patch in that space, divide the unit size by 2 (two squares per side in a four-patch) and then add the seam allowance: 1½ in. plus ½ in. equals 2 in., so you would cut 2-in. four-patch squares. Piece-o-cake, right?

I HAVE GOOD NEWS AND BAD NEWS

First, the bad news: For every traditional piecing method, there is at least one other way to accomplish the deed. For example, instead of making flying geese units with a quarter-square triangle and two half-square triangles, you can use a rectangle and two squares, *or* with the right tool you can cut all three shapes from strips, *or* you can make four flying geese units at once with five squares, one larger and four smaller, *or* you can turn two half-square triangle units into a flying geese unit. It can get confusing!

Quilter's Math

- Determine the size of the grid elements.
- Start with and stick with finished sizes while you do the math, then add back the seam allowance at the end.
- Don't forget the rules of thumb for quarter-square and half-square triangles.

So what?

Why bring up all this headache-inducing math in a book about bad things happening to good quilters? Have you ever lost a pattern with only half the blocks complete? Yeah, me too. You can use this system to evaluate the blocks you have, break down the elements based on a grid system, then do some quilter's math to solve the mystery!

Assemble the Block

Once the block parts are cut, arrange the block elements on your worktable. Start by sewing the subunits together, like the flying geese, nine-patch, and four-patches. Press according to the pattern instructions after sewing each seam, then replace the subunit in the block arrangement. Continue to assemble the subunits until you have a block arrangement that can be sewn into rows. The last step is sewing the block rows together. Check the size of the block once it's assembled. If it measures up, then make the next block. If not, check out the tips below to make some fixes.

To paraphrase a sage on blocks that are too large: *If thy block offends thee, cut it off!* No! Wait! Stop! Before you reach for the ruler and your handy-dandy rotary cutter to "true up" the block, take a look at the block and see if you can diagnose the problem. Simply trimming an oversized block can create more problems than it solves—particularly if the block includes elements that need to be considered in the seam allowances. Specifically, trimming a too-big block can compromise triangular-pieced points at the edges.

As for trimming or "truing up" the block—that is, placing a large ruler on top of the block and trimming the oversize block to size—some blocks, those that are symmetrical, can be trimmed to size as long as pieced points aren't compromised.

Unfortunately, the trim-down option isn't available if your block is too small. You can fudge or ease in undersize blocks as you sew the quilt together. If your block is too small, there can be a lot of fabric hiding in the seams. Grab your handy-dandy seam ripper, and learn the frog stitch (*rip it, rip it!*—yes, it's a bad joke).

SIZING ISSUES

My Block Is Too Big	My Block Is Too Small
Measure the parts: Were they cut accurately? If the parts are pieced and trimmed like half-square or quarter-square triangles, were they trimmed properly?	Block parts that are too small will result in a block that is too small.
Are the seams stretched so you can see the threads peeking through the piecing?	Make sure the pressing is crisp, leaving no flaps or gaps.
Check the seams. Most likely if the block is too big, one or more of the seam allowances will be too small.	Check the seams: If the block is too small, look for seams that need to go on a serious diet.

Checking Seam Allowances

To check seam allowances, find an acrylic ruler that has a really clear ¼-in. line. Place the ¼-in. line marking on the ruler directly over the sewn seam. You shouldn't see the edge of the fabric sticking out from under the ruler. If you do, the seam is too big. If you don't see any of the seam, but if the edge of the fabric is clearly visible under the ruler (and then some), your seam is too small. Adjust the needle position, or adjust the guide used to feed the pieces for sewing. And sew again. Making a test seam with scrap fabrics is highly recommended whenever you start a new sewing session.

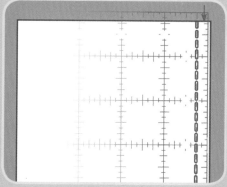

Seam is too large.

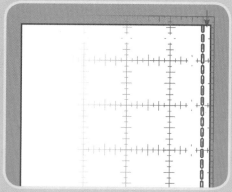

Seam is too small.

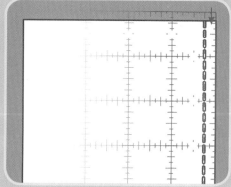

Seam is just right.

A problem with the dimension of a quilt block always comes down to one of three things: An accurate seam allowance, proper pressing technique, and cutting. Take a look before resorting to drastic rotary cutting measures. Turn the block over and look for some clues—it's like solving a mystery.

Bottom line: It's best to identify any cutting, pressing, or piecing issues early in the quilt construction. It simply isn't fun to fudge your way through the entire quilt assembly. A little bit off can create a heck of a mess if left alone. "A stitch in time, saves nine"—absolutely!

Furling, Popping, or Spinning

It goes by several names, including "that technique in the center of a four-patch." No matter what you call it, the concept is the same: Make a four-patch (or any block) so the row seams "nest," then pull out the last two or three stitches of the shorter seam at the point where they intersect. Then furl the seam allowance at the very center of the block. The result: The main part of the seams rotate

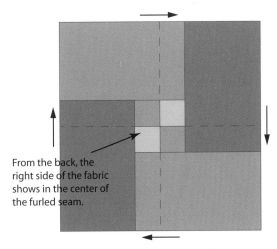

From the back, the right side of the fabric shows in the center of the furled seam.

Furling at the seam intersection opens and flattens a four-patch block where the seams come together.

clockwise or counterclockwise around the center of the block.

It's a great technique for several reasons:

- When sewing a series of four-patches side by side, the neighboring seams nest beautifully, as long as the four-patches have been fed into the sewing machine the same way each time.

- When multiple seams converge in the center of a block, like a pinwheel block, the block will be considerably less bulky at the center seam intersection if the seam is furled.

- Despite what you might think, this is a time-tested technique—used extensively in hand piecing—that won't weaken the quilt construction at the furled intersection.

- It applies to both hand- and machined-pieced blocks.

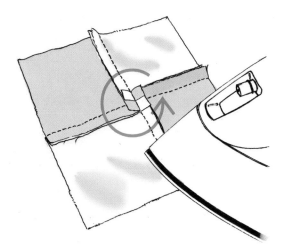

Press the seams from the back of the block first so the seam direction rotates around the center intersection.

Pin It!

Fabric stretches as it interacts with the presser foot, feed dogs, the sewing machine needle, and other fabric. Pins placed strategically along the to-be-sewn seam can reduce or eliminate misbehaving fabric. Pins are like having an extra hand in tight spot.

It's not a good idea to sew over pins. That implies that pins that cross over sewing lines should be removed as you sew. As the pin is removed, the fabric shifts and, if you aren't careful, seams distort. Similarly, if the pin hits a metal quarter-inch guide on the side of the sewing machine foot, the seam can jiggle to the left or to the right.

For an accurate, consistent, pin-friendly seam:

- Use sharp, very fine pins. Be sure to discard bent pins, and replace your pin collection with new pins every couple of months or as needed.
- Place the pin on the inside of the stitching more than ¼ in. away from the fabric edge, so there's no chance that the sewing machine needle will interact with the pins (A).

It's also a good idea to secure seam allowances that "nest" on both sides of the seam intersection. That means placing two pins, one on either side of the seam intersection, which, if done correctly, can be time consuming (B). As an alternative, place a pin on the inside of the stitching so it crosses over the seam intersection and stabilizes both sides of the nested seam allowance (C). Or use a fork-shaped pin to secure both seams with one double-pointed pin.

To keep from sewing over a point, like the tip of a flying geese unit, sew the seam so the unit with the point on top, so you can watch as you sew the seam that it doesn't cut off the point (D).

If you are sewing a seam where two points meet, use a pin to stab straight though both points, then secure the seam with a pin on either side of the point to avoid slipping. Sometimes strategically pressed seams can also keep the points accurate.

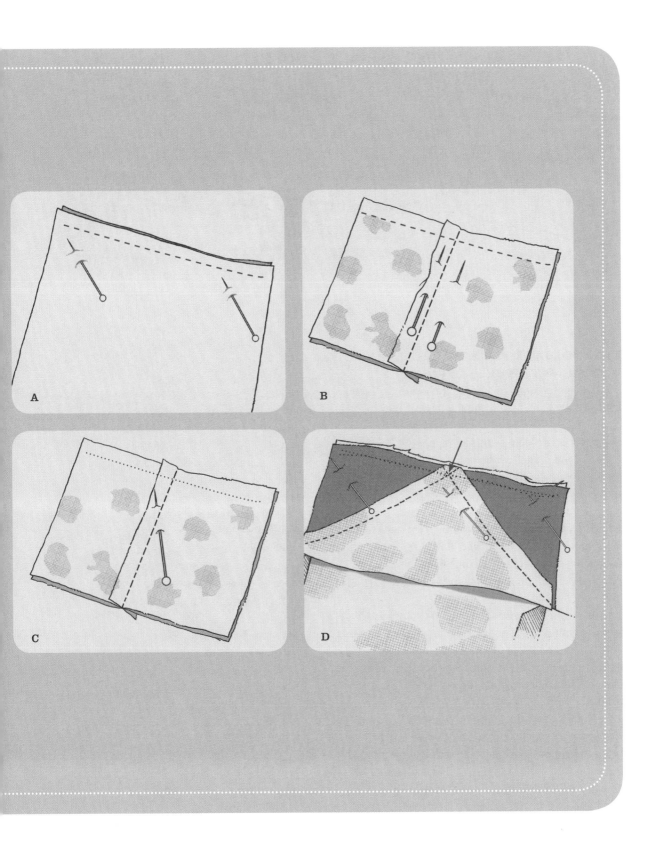

A

B

C

D

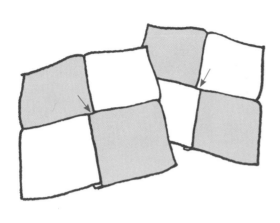

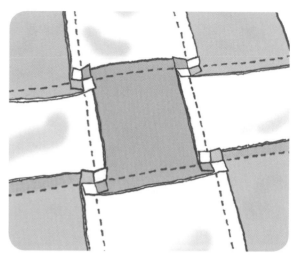

A gap, or overlap at the seam intersection will keep the seam from furling properly.

You can furl the seam intersections on a nine-patch block, too!

HOW TO MAKE FOUR-PATCH BLOCKS WITH FURLED SEAMS

Sew two-patch units and press the seams consistently to one side, usually toward the darker fabric. Sew pairs of two-patches with opposing fabric facing and seams nested.

Be sure to feed the four-patches into the sewing machine exactly the same each time—that is, the light fabric first or the dark fabric first.

Using a seam ripper, remove the last two or three stitches from the two-patch seam on each side of the four-patch unit. Stop removing stitches at the intersection with the longer four-patch seam.

Press from the back so the seams rotate and the center intersection is furled. Note that only the center of the block seam section is open; the rest of the seams are pressed to one side, each rotating around the center. Press from the front.

Seams can furl clockwise or counter-clockwise. Also notice that a clockwise seam rotation from the back is counterclockwise from the front. The secret isn't that the seams furl one way or another; it's that they all furl in the same direction.

> **TIP:** Sometimes, the first time you really have the chance to step back and look at the entire quilt without being nose-to-the-grindstone into sewing the seams is when the quilt is sandwiched for basting. On more than one occasion, I've unbasted a quilt to remove and replace a block because it was sewn wrong or it was simply the wrong color. I figure, at this stage, after putting in plenty of hours of sewing, I want no regrets. I've been equally inspired to find a mistake and let it stay in the quilt.

What could possibly go wrong? If your seams won't furl, take a closer look at the original seam intersection. Where the two two-patches nest, was the seam intersection spot-on? If the seam intersections overlap, or if there is a gap at the center—even a little bit in either case, the seam won't twist.

Does furling only apply to four-patch-type blocks? No; however, seams must be pressed alternately across a row as well as in the neighboring row to be able to furl across the entire long seam.

Fixing Mistakes

Nobody likes to make a mistake. When a quilter makes a mistake on a project, several options emerge: Fix it, abandon it, or let it be. We'll get to "the fix" in a minute.

Sometimes, the fix isn't obvious. Or the corrective action is so convoluted that it's not worth the physical or emotional effort needed.

Quilters have a way of making light of an error once it has been discovered. Let's face it, we're not perfect. We like to laugh, and we love a good story. Sometimes the best comedy routine is right in your own studio, documented for all the world to see in your quilt.

 ## Modern Quilting

My friend Carolyn Friedlander (carolynfriedlander.com), modern quilter extraordinaire, offers some tips to ease you into this brave new modern quilty world. Her comments might surprise you. She says:

"Here are the basic things that I think you should know about 'modern.' First, know that how I describe modern is only my opinion and the way that I choose to see it. What I find to be interesting about modern is that you are likely to find other perspectives depending on whom you ask. While this might seem overwhelming (and possibly confusing), I think it is great because it perfectly illustrates one of my favorite things about it, which is that you can make it whatever you want it to be. How liberating is that?

"I like to think of modern quilting as an *attitude* toward making things rather than a specific *style*. That attitude to me is represented as an openness to trying new things, an interest in conveying your own personal story, and the decision to quilt (and make things in general) by choice because you enjoy and value it.

"You can erase all notions of what a quilt should look like and, instead, take out your sketchbook to start drawing some ideas of your own. Grab some fabric that inspires you, and start sewing."

Sometimes, the quilt that offers challenges and detours in its construction might be the most frustrating to create, but ends up being the one that stretches and satisfies you. Have you ever heard a quilter say, "I'll never make a quilt like that one again, but I have to admit, it's one of my favorites"? Maybe you've said it yourself.

FIX IT

When you decide that a correction is in order, it's easier than you might think to remove a small portion of the quilt, make the correction, and replace it, particularly if the quilt isn't sandwiched or quilted yet. Here's how:

First, locate and mark the mistake. Then, turn the quilt wrong side up and, with a seam ripper, pull out all four seams connecting the misplaced block or element (plus at least 1 in. of the seams on adjoining sides), following the original row and block piecing configuration. This will create a square- or rectangular-shaped hole in the quilt, with adjoining seams unsewn.

Replace or adjust the mistake in its proper position, and with the right sides together, pin one side of the corrected block into place. Sew a ¼-in. seam allowance. Pull the extra quilt material out of the way, and start sewing the opposite, parallel seam in place in a similar manner, using pins as needed. Then sew the two perpendicular seams, pinning and nesting the seam intersections as necessary. Press the repaired seams, first from the back, then from the front of the quilt top.

To avoid stretching the fabric, proceed carefully when removing stitches along any bias seam. If the problem is with one side of a half-square triangle unit, consider removing the pieced square unit, then removing the triangle before sewing a new one in place.

The Thrill of Piecing and the Agony of Appliqué

Appliqué has an unfortunate reputation. Some quilters, especially new quilters, think appliqué is difficult, and they much prefer piecing. Consider that hand sewing the folded edge of a binding to the back of a quilt is almost the same skill as hand sewing an appliqué shape to the background fabric. Okay, so there might be a few extra steps to appliqué, but the basic skills are the same.

Appliqué adds dimension and opens a whole new world of shapes to your quilt. As with most every quilting technique, you have lots of options.

MACHINE APPLIQUÉ

Using interfacing

Fusible interfacing is a very lightweight nonwoven fabric that is smooth on one side and has a heat-sensitive glue, or fusible material, on the other. The interfacing becomes part of the quilt's construction.

Using a permanent fabric marking pen, trace the appliqué shape onto the smooth side of the interfacing. The traced shape should be drawn as it will appear on the quilt, not reversed. Cut a slit in the center of the shape to be used for turning later, and then roughly trim the interfacing around the shape. Place the right side of the fabric selected for the appliqué shape facing the fusible (not smooth) side of the interfacing. Secure the interfacing to the shape with a few pins.

With the interfacing facing up, sew directly on the traced line all the way around the shape (see the top left photo on the facing page).

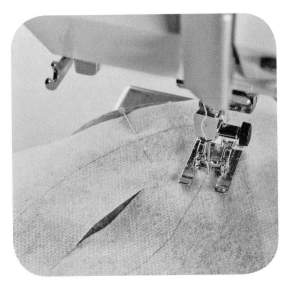

With the fusible interfacing pinned to the fabric, sew directly on the drawn line.

Turn the shape right side out through the slit in the interfacing.

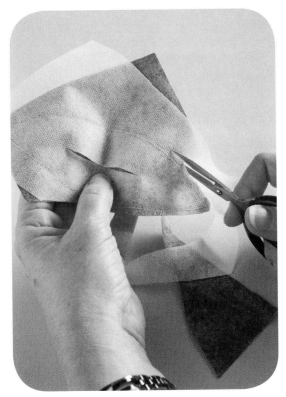

Trim fabric and interfacing about ⅛ in. away from the sewn line.

Then trim both layers of fabric about ⅛ in. away from the sewing line (see photo at left).

Turn the shape right side out through the slit in the center. A blunt knitting needle or chopstick works wonders—just don't poke through the interfacing (see photo above)!

Place the appliqué shape on the background fabric, with fusible interfacing facing the right side of the background; arrange the shape as directed in the pattern, then fuse the appliqué shape onto the background with a hot, steamy iron. Sew around the appliqué shape with a zigzag, satin, or blanket stitch, using matching or contrasting thread, depending on the look you want to achieve. Use an open-toed foot for any of these stitches.

Sticky Secrets

With either fusible interfacing or fusible web, the key ingredient is heat-activated glue. To keep from getting the fusible glue on the surface of the iron, many quilters like to use a heat-resistant pressing cloth or sheet inserted between the iron and the appliqué shapes. The fusible glue won't stick to the pressing sheet, and the iron stays clean.

However, the fusible material adheres better to the fabric with a puff of steam from the iron. If you apply steam with a pressing sheet in place, you are only squirting steam onto the pressing sheet, which reflects it back onto the iron. You need to remove the pressing sheet to add the steam.

If you find that a little bit of the fusible material adheres to the iron, don't worry. The surface of the iron is easily cleaned with an iron cleaner obtained at the fabric store. Just follow the package instructions.

Try not to get the fusible glue on your ironing board cover. It won't come off easily and will adhere to clean fabric or blocks at the most inopportune times. If you get fusible material on the ironing board cover, cover the spot with a paper towel or piece of scrap fabric, then rub the fabric with a hot iron. The clean fabric should accept most of the fusible material, but you may have to repeat the process a few times, each time with a clean piece of cloth.

Using fusible web

Fusible web is a paper-backed heat-sensitive adhesive. For fusible appliqué, you want the light, sew-through variety.

Be careful—some fusible web shouldn't be used for sewing! The adhesives on the heavier fusibles will gum up your sewing machine.

Using a permanent fabric marking pen, trace the appliqué shape in *reverse* onto the paper side of the fusible web. Roughly trim the paper around the shape and cut a slit in the center of the shape. Then cut away the center of the shape, about ¼ in. away from the line. With a hot iron, fuse the roughly trimmed shape to the wrong side of the appliqué fabric.

Trim the appliqué shape on the traced line, and place the appliqué shape on the background fabric. The fusible web on the appliqué should be facing the right side of the background fabric. Arrange as indicated in your pattern. Remove the paper, and then fuse the appliqué shape onto the background with a hot, steamy iron. Sew around the appliqué shape with a zigzag, satin, or blanket stitch, using matching or contrasting thread, depending on the look you want to achieve. Use an open-toed foot for any of these stitches.

HAND APPLIQUÉ

In my mind, the only way to do hand appliqué is the back basting method. The one downside of this method is that the pattern is traced in its entirety on the back of the base fabric, so a pattern that includes the entire shape arrangement, not just a flower petal here and a stem there, is best.

Trace the appliqué shape in reverse onto the back of the base fabric (see the left photo below). Cut the fabric for the appliqué shape slightly larger than the pattern appliqué shape (see the right photo below).

Pin the appliqué fabric to the right side of the base fabric, right side up, so that the appliqué fabric covers the lines plus at least a ⅛-in. seam allowance (preferably a bit more). Hold the fabrics to a light source to be sure all lines plus seam allowances are adequately planned.

From the wrong side of the base fabric, pin-baste roughly around the shape using appliqué pins. Also from the wrong side of the base fabric, using a heavy thread in a high-contrast color and a thicker needle, sew a tight running stitch (about 10 stitches to the inch) directly onto the line to secure the appliqué to the block. Don't knot the thread at the beginning or end of the running stitch, and stitch all the way around the shape. From the front, trim the appliqué fabric about ⅛ in. from the running stitch; leave the running stitch in place for at least an hour, or overnight.

Then, working from the front, and using an appliqué needle and a very fine cotton thread in a color that matches the appliqué shape, pull out a few of the running stitches. Bend the appliqué seam allowance under and secure

(Continued on p. 56)

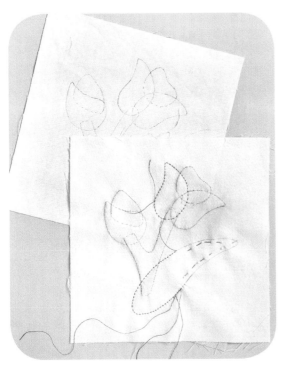

Trace the appliqué shape in reverse onto the back of the base fabric.

From the front, trim the appliqué fabric about ⅛ in. from the running stitch.

🧵 A Few Tips for Your Hand-Appliqué Project

Once the appliqué shape has been basted to the front of the background fabric, you might encounter some challenges. Here are a few pointers to save the day.

- **Inside points** (like the dip in the top of a Valentine heart): Don't start on the inside point, but start along a gentle curve similar to the way you'd approach a pointy point. Snip the seam allowance right up to, but not crossing, the basting stitches. As you approach the inside point, turn the seam allowance under as before and secure it, but use caution, because as the seam allowance gets smaller, it is more likely to fray (A). With one side of the inside point secured, take one deep stitch into the point, then take a second stitch on top of it (B). Proceed as before along the opposite side of the point (C).

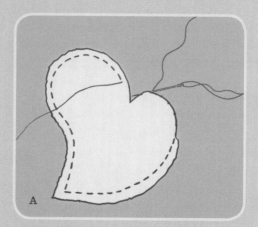

A

- **Inner curves**: Snip the seam allowance up to, but not past, the basting stitch. If the curve is severe, more snips at shorter intervals are needed. Snipping the seam on an inside curve will make turning the seam allowance under the shape easier (D).

- **Pointy points**: If you are securing a shape that has a pointy point, don't start with the point. Instead, start turning the applique along a gentle curve or straightaway. As you approach the point, turn under and secure the appliqué shape all the way to the point, and take a

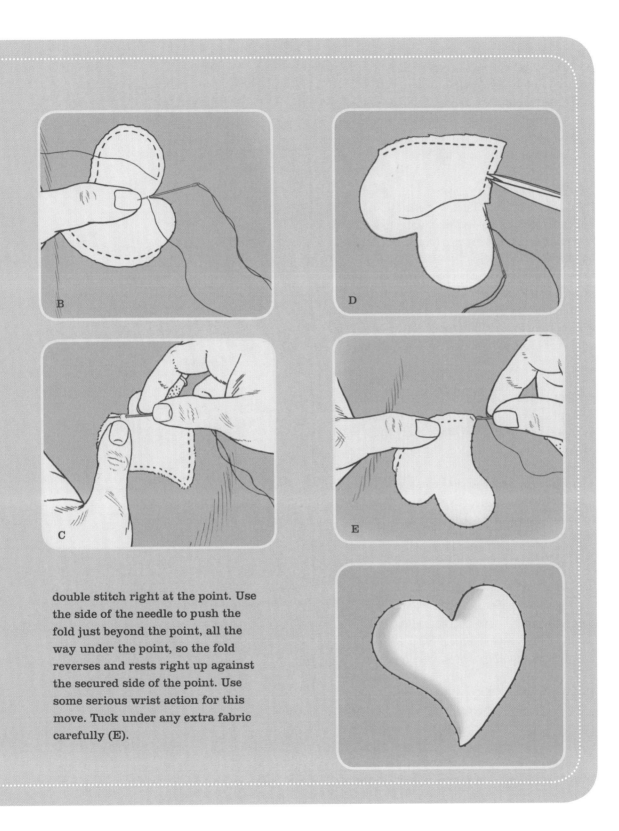

double stitch right at the point. Use the side of the needle to push the fold just beyond the point, all the way under the point, so the fold reverses and rests right up against the secured side of the point. Use some serious wrist action for this move. Tuck under any extra fabric carefully (E).

(Continued from p. 53)

the fold to the background fabric with short appliqué stitches that *just* catch the fold of the shape (see the photo below).

Proceed around the appliqué shape, pulling out the running stitches about ½ in. ahead of where you are securing the appliqué. Add pieces one at a time until the block is complete.

PAPER PIECING

Perfect points, tons of detail, but all that paper. Paper piecing—sewing fabric to paper, one piece at a time—makes blocks that look very bizarre during the *process* of making the blocks, but results in beautiful quilts with shapes that would be nearly impossible using mathematically correct piecing techniques.

Beware of a few things that could go wrong in a paper-pieced project:

- Make sure the fabric completely covers the paper shape with added fabric real estate for seam allowances. If not, the block will have a hole. As a result, the fabric piece must be removed and replaced, or the hole repaired.

- To make the paper easy to remove when the quilt is complete, decrease the stitch length to about 1.5 on the sewing machine setting. Normal piecing is usually between 2.0 and 2.5.

- Change the needle often, not so much because the paper dulls the point of the needle, but because decreasing the stitch length means the needle pierces the paper and fabric more frequently, dulling it.

- Leave the paper backing on the blocks until the entire quilt is pieced or at least until the block is sewn into the quilt on all of its sides.

- A slight diagonal pull on the finished block will help release the paper from the blocks.

TIP: Basting with a heavier needle and thread will have left a perforation in the appliqué fabric that will allow the seam allowance to turn exactly where you want it.

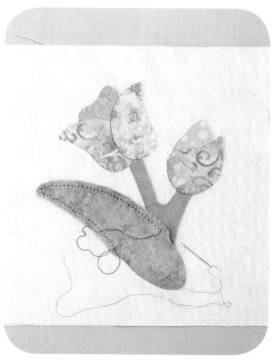

Bend the appliqué seam allowance under and secure the fold to the base fabric.

- Water-soluble paper products that have been designed for this technique may create a nice alternative to paper (which has to be removed by hand).

HAND PIECING

I used to think that "handwork" meant hand quilting or hand embroidery exclusively. For some reason, the prospect of hand piecing never entered my mind; piecing by machine was so fast and so much fun. When the local quilt shop offered a class in hand piecing, I enrolled.

Hand piecing might take a little longer than machine piecing, but it's just as accurate, if not more so. It's relaxing, and it's portable. Any block can be hand-pieced. Some blocks are easier to make by hand, especially when curves or set-in Y-seams are involved.

For some solid advice on the world of hand piecing, I turned to a good friend. Sharon Stroud (sharonstroud.com) is a quilter, author, and teacher. She knows a thing or two about hand piecing.

The bliss of hand piecing

Hand piecing can be done anywhere, anytime. It's portable, quiet, easy, and can be done in found bits of time. Here are some tips for success from Sharon:

Thread: Use only about 18 in. of thread; a shorter length will tangle and knot less than a longer piece. Match the thread color to the darker fabric. To sew a white patch and a black patch, use black thread. Sometimes a shade of gray will match most of your fabrics, but don't skimp—stitches that show are distracting. My choice is a 50-wt. cotton.

Needles: Sharps size 11 are my favorites for hand piecing. They are easy to hold and can be "loaded" with a fair number of stitches before pulling the needle through. They are thin and pierce the fabric easily. Change your needle

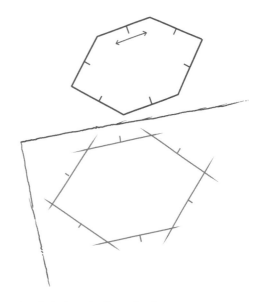

For hand piecing, whether using freezer paper or template plastic, transferring the exact shape before seam allowances is key.

after about eight hours of sewing. A dull needle causes stress to the hand and wrist.

Transferring the pattern: Mark with a tool that you can easily see on the wrong side of the fabric. Trace around the template, including any match marks. With freezer paper templates (pressed onto the wrong side of your fabric with a hot, dry iron), a ruler can be used to extend the seam lines to form crosshairs at the points.

If using template plastic, it is easier to place a small dot at the corners of the shape, then draw the lines between the dots.

Place the fabric on fine-grit sandpaper to stabilize it for tracing. Because we are working on the wrong side of the fabric, the pattern will be reversed. Blocks that are symmetrical won't be affected, but letters and numbers need to be reversed for your templates.

The first step is to transfer each exact shape without seam allowances to the fabric. Cut out the shape with scissors or a rotary cutter and ruler, leaving a 1/4-in. seam allowance on each side of each piece.

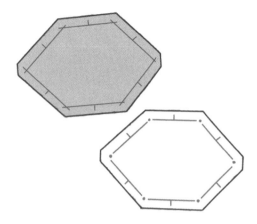

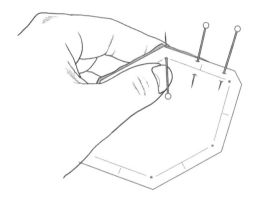

Once the shape is transferred to the wrong side of the fabric, including match marks, dots, and crosshairs, cut the fabric ¼ in. away from the shape.

Select the first seam to sew. Before taking a stitch, align both ends of the seam and match marks with fine pins. Then pin the seam to secure it.

Sewing: Sew from "dot to dot" or "crosshair to crosshair," not from raw edge to raw edge, as in machine piecing. This allows seam allowances to be pressed to best advantage at the seam intersections. Start and end the lines of stitching at the dots (crosshairs).

- Place the two fabrics right sides together with the seam to be sewn aligned.

- Before taking a stitch, align the corners and match marks front to back with fine pins.

- Start sewing with a knot and a backstitch; end with a double backstitch.

- Only sew through two layers of fabric.

- Never sew into the seam allowances.

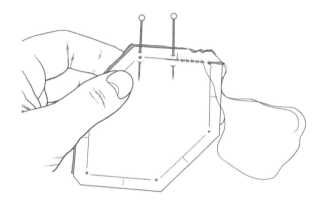

With a quilter's knot in the thread, start a line of stitching with a backstitch, then load the needle with several small running stitches along the seam line.

Backstitch before starting a new needleful of stitches. Always check the back before pulling the needle through; if the needle does not follow the drawn seams front to back, pull the needle out, repin, and stitch again. If you pull the needle through and discover a problem, you need to unthread the needle, rip out the stitches, and start over.

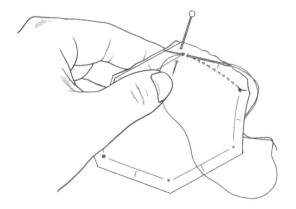

To complete the seam, backstitch and park the needle before aligning and sewing an adjacent next seam or double back stitch to end and break the thread.

When you encounter a seam intersection blocking your way across a seam, backstitch immediately before the intersection, then pass through the seam allowance directly through the crosshairs. Only sew through two layers of fabric at a time, so if more than one seam intersection blocks your way, pass through each, one at a time, sending the needle directly through the crosshairs. Once you're onto the next seam, backstitch before proceeding.

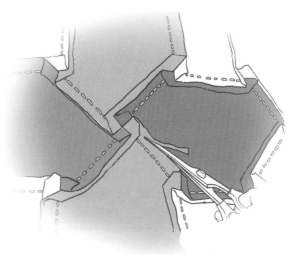

After the seams are pressed, trim away about 1/16 in. of any dark fabric in the seam that might shadow through to the front of the quilt.

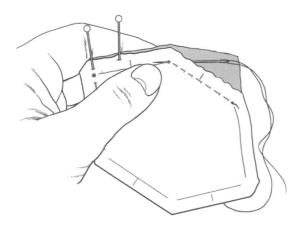

At a seam intersection, pass the needle through the seam end points, and pull the thread firmly for precise points.

Pressing: Because of the point-to-point sewing, it is easy to press hand-pieced seam allowances to best advantage rather than to the "dark side." Try to isolate each seam as you press it. Press first from the wrong side of the block, easing seams into position. Then press from the right side.

Grading: After the block is pressed, "grade" dark seam allowances so that they do not shadow under lighter patches. Remove about 1/16 in. from the dark seam allowance layer. The block will be easier to quilt with no risk of dark shadows.

You will be amazed at how easy hand piecing is and how quickly finished blocks accumulate. Ahhh . . . feel that bliss!

How to Make a Quilter's Knot

- Thread the needle as usual.
- Hold the needle in your dominant hand, form an X with the end of the thread and the needle, and pinch the needle and thread end between your thumb and index finger.
- While holding the thread end with your finger, wrap the thread around the needle two or three times counter clockwise, then pinch the loops in between your thumb and index finger while pulling the needle and the length of thread all the way to the end.

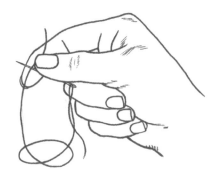

Hold needle between thumb and index finger. Place the thread end on top to form an X.

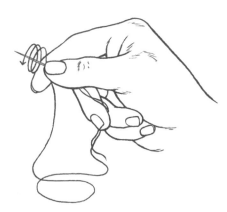

Squeeze thumb and finger to hold the end, then wrap the needle with the thread three times counterclockwise.

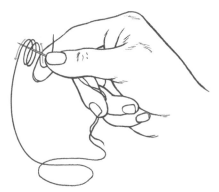

Pull the wound thread until the thread end is very short, then pinch the thread loops with thumb and index finger and pull the needle through.

Ready, Set, Sew!

Now that you've got your blocks sewn, let's get going on sewing your quilt top together.

Under Construction

Once you have made or collected a bunch of blocks, it's time to arrange them into a quilt. As we've seen already, options abound. Use a design wall, or clear the coffee table out of the center of the living room. Evict the cat and the dog temporarily while your next quilt creation is under construction.

Add sashing and cornerstones between the blocks to calm complicated piecing and prints.

Add sashing and cornerstones between the blocks. Soften the impact of harsh secondary patterns or create a neutral resting place for the eye to absorb the detail in the piecing and appliqué. Add glamour to the sashing and cornerstones with some piecing or appliqué techniques.

A simple arrangement of blocks sewn into rows is an easy way to complete a quilt top.

Blocks can be arranged side by side in rows. Even the simplest blocks can make interesting secondary patterns when arranged this way. Add one or more borders, or take the blocks straight to the edge of the quilt. All the blocks need to be the same size for this to work seamlessly (pun intended).

Sashing without cornerstones can really draw attention to the blocks.

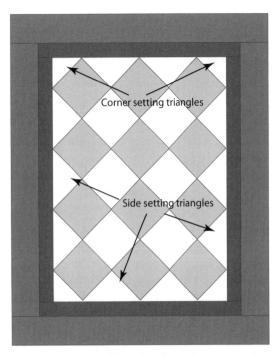

Blocks set on point add another dimension to the quilt. Setting triangles should be planned so the fabric grain follows the outer edge of the quilt center.

You can also add sashing without cornerstones. Usually, vertical sashing strips are placed between the blocks, then long horizontal sashing strips are sewn between the rows. Be careful to align vertical block seams as the horizontal sashing strips are pinned and sewn. Otherwise, the blocks may appear to wiggle back and forth on the quilt.

Arrange the blocks on point, and add setting triangles around the outside edge of the quilt. Beware that arranging the blocks on point can increase the size of the quilt quickly. A lap-size quilt can graduate quickly to a queen size or larger when the blocks are sewn on point. Things get a little complicated when calculating the size of the setting triangles. To keep the straight-of-grain along the outer edge of the quilt, the corner-setting triangles are half-square triangles and the side-setting triangles are quarter-square triangles.

What's the Magic Number?

The magic number is 1.414. What is so special about this number? It has to do with geometry, and algebra, and brain-numbing formulas.

Without getting too technical, for the corner half-square triangles, take the finished size of the block (12 in., for example) and divide by 1.414, round, and add ⅞ in. Cut two squares, then cut once on the diagonal. For the side-setting triangles, start with the finished size of the block (12 in.) and multiply by 1.414, round, and add 1¼ in. Cut a square of fabric that size, then cut twice on the diagonal to make four side-setting triangles. Repeat until you get the correct number of triangles.

I rarely make my setting triangles this way. Why? Because the squares are just too large! For example: A side-setting triangle for a 12-in. block is over 18 in. square. I don't have a ruler that big. Sure, I could use more than one ruler at a time, but the risk that I'll mess up the cutting and end up with the wrong size triangle is real. To start all over again is a significant fabric investment.

I love math, and I love quilt blocks set on point. But if I have to remember when to multiply or divide weird numbers, my hair starts to set on fire.

To keep the smoldering to a minimum, I prefer to look at the setting triangles as one super-size straight border. That way, all I have to do is determine how wide that border is, add an inch or two to make the blocks "float," then cut half-square and quarter-square triangles using the 45-degree and 90-degree lines on my ruler.

Here's another formula: Take the size of the block (12 in. in the example) and square it, or multiply the number by itself: 12 x 12 = 144. Divide that number by 2 for 72, then take the square root (a button to push on most standard calculators), which rounds to 8½ in. Add at least 1½ in. or more to make the blocks float

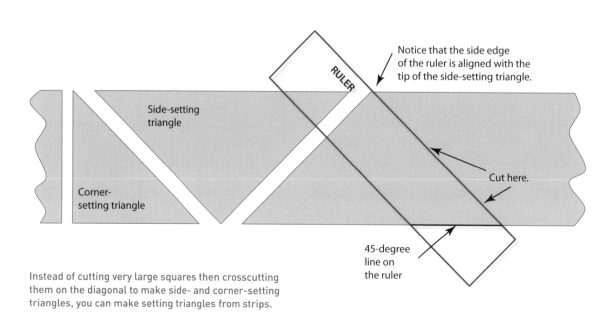

Instead of cutting very large squares then crosscutting them on the diagonal to make side- and corner-setting triangles, you can make setting triangles from strips.

away from the edge of the quilt center. Use the 45-degree and 90-degree lines on the ruler to cut the strip into half-square and quarter-square setting triangles. This oversimplifies the math, leaving some trimming to do, but it works and it's easy.

Using the same concept of cutting the setting triangles from fabric strips, Marti Michell has a great tool, the Diagonal Set Triangle Ruler, that takes all of the math out of the picture. If you know the size of the block, the lines on the ruler provide the strip width. I recommend it! Plus, the tool is more technically accurate than my fly-by-the-seat-of-the-pants method described above, because it incorporates seam allowance calculations.

Whose Blocks Are These?

It's one thing to make a set of quilt blocks yourself, realizing that a seam is a little off here or a piece of fabric is sewn upside down there. They're your blocks, you made them, and you accept them with all their little quirks and personality disorders. Just like your in-laws.

It's quite another to receive blocks made by someone else—the result of a garage sale find, a block exchange, or a group quilt project—and find quirks and mistakes.

When given a set of rules, it's inevitable that quilters, working on their own, will interpret the rules *creatively*. If you're the one in charge of making a quilt from blocks that aren't quite, shall we say, constructed in accordance with generally accepted quilting practices, you could be in for a rough ride.

Instead of painstakingly reconstructing the errant quilt blocks (taking out someone else's stitches feels a little like haunting their creative spirit), perhaps there's another solution.

TIP: This trick will work in lots of circumstances. Small prints hide many evils. Solids or large-scale prints could draw attention to them.

If you opt for a simple quilt construction—blocks, sashing, cornerstones—for blocks that vary in size slightly, select a sashing fabric with a fussy miniature print. Cut the sashing as if the blocks are all the same size. For example, if most of the blocks are a 12-in. finished size, cut the sashing strips 12 in. long by whatever sashing width you've decided fits with the block arrangement. If one or more of the blocks are a little less than the requisite 12-in. size, add a small border of the fussy sashing fabric on one, two, three, or all four sides of the too-small block, making the block a bit larger than needed. Then trim the block to the requisite 12½-in. unfinished size. Keep as much of the original block construction intact as you can, and try not to compromise any points with trimming or seams. Once the "fixed" block is set with the rest of the blocks, the fussy sashing strips will match the corrected block, and you won't even notice that the block was too small to begin with.

If one of the blocks is too large, perhaps it'll work as the quilt's label on the back. And of course, there's always the option to turn it into the world's largest, most exquisite pot holder.

The MIL Quilt

I had been quilting four or five years when a knock came at my door. It was my neighbor, Sherri. After a long illness, her mother-in-law (the "MIL") passed away.

In her belongings, the MIL had had a quilt, partially constructed. Sherri presented me with the box full of blocks and fabric pieces, and very little else except for a few scribbled notes, a rough sketch of the quilt concept, and lots of yellow sticky notes.

Some of the blocks were sewn into rows with sashing strips in between, but block and sashing sizes were not consistent. The fabrics were lovely— colorful Caribbean-style prints that looked like they could have been hand-dyed, probably purchased on a memorable vacation. Clearly, the MIL did the best she could with what she had. And you could feel her enthusiasm for the project mixed in with the process missteps. What to do?

I wanted to preserve as much of the MIL's sewing as I could, but more blocks needed to be sewn into rows. I decided I would use the blocks, but had to unsew the rows and sashing strips to have enough fabric to complete the quilt. I trimmed the blocks and sashing strips to a consistent size and pieced the quilt into rows of blocks, sashing, and cornerstones.

Once trimmed, the blocks and sashing strips went together beautifully. I found a border print that didn't match the original fabrics perfectly, but blended with all the Caribbean colors. A few months later, I presented the completed quilt to Sherri, and she was thrilled!

Sherri had planned to give the quilt to the MIL's sister, but after seeing it, she ended up keeping it. And, I think the finished quilt helped Sherri resolve some lingering issues with her MIL. Even a quilt fill of missteps can be so much more than just a quilt.

Finishing: Border Issues

The quilt center is complete, and the end is in sight. The countdown begins! Once the quilt center is done, I actually start a mental countdown of the remaining seams. Adding the border is only four seams away from a completed quilt top.

Slap on a border and call it good, right? Well, maybe. Some quilts call for a little something extra. Most of the time, I prefer to resist the urge to finish the quilt with a single border.

Remove the Ruffle

The border is on and the quilt is done! Lay the quilt flat on the floor or hang it on the design wall and step back to appreciate your work. And there it is. No mistaking it. A ripple. The border looks more like a ruffle than an extension of the quilt. And it's noticeable. What could be wrong?

If the quilt's border has a little extra poof where there should be no poof at all, then the border is probably longer than the quilt top. Unfortunately, the poof won't correct itself, and if you continue on and ignore the issue, the finished quilt will likely not lie flat or hang square on the wall. Worse, quilting through the extra fabric might cause unappealing folds or pleat-like areas along the quilt's edge.

Remove the border or borders, measure again, then replace the remeasured and trimmed border on the quilt. Before you throw up your hands in despair and commit the near-complete quilt to the UFO closet of horrors, consider this: At most, we're talking about reconstructing four seams. *Four*. Yes, they are big seams, but how many hundreds of seams make up the quilt center? Don't bother counting; guaranteed, it's a lot more than four. Considering all of the work that went into your quilt, this is an easy fix, and a worthwhile one.

Deflate the Volcano

When you lay the finished quilt top flat and notice that the borders hit the floor first and the rest of the quilt center follows, leaving a mountain (or a molehill) of fabric floating above the floor, then the borders are likely too small. If the quilt doesn't lie flat, it may make sense to remove the borders and add a bit more fabric before determining the final borders' sizes.

Sometimes, the volcano is the result of too-small borders converging in the center. Re-evaluate the seam allowances and take corrective seam reconstruction action.

It's Hip to Be Square

There is one other possibility—that the quilt center isn't square (by *square*, I mean that it doesn't have 90-degree corners). A seam allowance here, a cutting issue there, pressing off a little bit here and there—it can add up! It's one thing if this "little bits here and there" concept is consistent throughout the quilt construction, but if construction problems are here, there, everywhere—like Old McDonald's Farm—you'll be singing a sour tune when it comes to those last few steps.

When it seems the only solution is to start over, drastic measures are in order. Sometimes a little trim to square up the corner edges of the quilt will be less noticeable than a border that's off significantly. It might take a couple of tries to remove only a very small slice from part of the quilt edge to create enough of a fix to complete the project. Unfortunately, if the trimmed border is pieced, some of the points might be compromised. So, it's a tradeoff—a quick fix with points at risk, or unsew and resew a whole lot of pieces—and it's your call.

Uh-ohh

You know that sinking feeling you get when you look at the amount of fabric you have and the amount of fabric you need and the two amounts don't quite match. The amount you have is just a little bit less than the amount you need. Here's a handy chart of do's and don'ts to use when you see the writing on the design wall.

WHAT TO DO WHEN RUNNING LOW ON FABRIC?

Do	Don't
Jump in the car and head to the quilt shop with a scrap of the fabric to see if you can find a match.	Pull it. It won't stretch. Really, it won't.
Send a group email to your quilty friends with a digital photo of the fabric, and beg for one small strip, or maybe two or three.	Call the quilt shop and describe the fabric: "It's blue with flowers on it; very pretty. I bought it three years ago. I bought it the same week my sister moved to a new apartment. Surely, you remember, right?"
Determine that your quilt would look so much better with cornerstones.	Find the fabric and buy 3 yd. of it when all you need is a 6-in. strip—just in case it happens again.
Consider an altogether different fabric for the border, even though it means some reverse sewing is in your future.	Cry. It won't help. I've tried. Cursing—same result.
Embrace your inner rebel and replace one end of one border with a handful of flying geese to coordinate with the quilt center.	Spray it with water and pull a little bit along the bias.
Border? What border? This was all part of a master plan—you really wanted that fabric for a table runner.	Bury it in a pot of soil and water it. Sorry, the cotton was done growing when it was picked.

Distilling the Mystery in Mitering

That last border stage of the quilt can be rather tedious. You schlep the whole quilt back and forth on the sewing table, first on the cutting table while borders are measured, one at a time, then under the sewing machine to attach them, one at a time. Side. Side. Top. Bottom. Side. Side. Top. Bottom. Each border is sewn one at a time the traditional way.

From the completion of my very first quilt, I have always appreciated mitered borders on quilts. Especially when striped fabrics are involved, that angled seam at the corner frames the quilt with a snappy look.

Mitered borders look so polished, they must be difficult to do, thought the novice quilter that I was. That's all I needed to propel me into wanting to know more. Why not?

Turns out, mitered borders are easier than traditionally pieced borders, especially when the quilt has multiple borders. It takes a bit more fabric to do mitered borders than it does to piece them traditionally. And you just have to get past that set-in seam. And practice. The Miter Touch Quilt on p. 100 walks you through the steps and the requisite practice so you can miter like a pro.

Lengthwise Grain

If I had my druthers, I'd cut all my quilt borders along the lengthwise grain—in other words, the long edge of the border that runs parallel to the selvage. This is the least stretchy cutting option, and it makes the last few steps of construction and the finished quilt top more stable. If you start with a piece of fabric off the bolt that is as long or longer than the longest side of the quilt, and the final border is less than 8 in. to 10 in. wide, then you'll have lots of extra fabric left over from the 40 in. of usable fabric width. One option to save fabric waste or scrap is to cut the binding strips along the lengthwise grain from the border fabric, but some prefer that the binding create a contrasting color finish to the quilt.

When cutting strips along the lengthwise grain, take the same precautions used to cut strips across the width-of-grain.

Quilt the Quilt

So you've finished your quilt top and everything looks as it should—there's just one more step: Time to quilt!

Quilt It

Congratulations! Your quilt top is finished. Aren't you ecstatic? You should be. That's a big accomplishment, and it came from your creativity—practically from thin air.

And you are scared out of your mind. You've got to quilt this thing, and all of a sudden the infamous UFO shelves in the closet are calling your name. That closet might be a pretty good place to stow the quilt top until you gather the gumption to quilt it.

The word *can't* keeps swirling around in your brain until you are paralyzed by the thought of having to quilt the quilt. What if you ruin it? What if you don't? Ruin it, that is.

I suppose if you don't quilt it, the quilt top will store nicely in that closet for years to come. Fold the quilt top a few times so it fits on a hanger like a pair of pants folded at the knee. Since there's no batting to worry about yet, foldlines will be pressed out before the quilt is sandwiched. Fold the quilt top with right sides together to reduce the potential for the pieces to fade. Someday, someone will open that closet and find it, your masterpiece, and wonder what kept you from finishing it. Maybe they'll quilt it, or send it out to be quilted by someone else, or donate it to a good cause, or give it to the neighbor down the street. Or, horror of all horrors, they might they throw it away. Let's not go there.

Confront the Demons

I understand why many quilters get intimidated by the last few steps of the quilt-making process. The voices in your head can work against you. And they can be very convincing. But here are some helpful rebuttals to help quiet those doubts.

Like solving any big problem, if you break down the project into basic steps, the task is much more approachable. Let's take a closer look at each step and see if we can't make this part of making a quilt a little more fun.

 Secret Signature

Before she sandwiches her quilt, my friend Amy always takes one extra step. She writes her name clearly on one of the seam allowances with a permanent fabric marker. Amy makes lots of quilts, and they are meant to be used, and used up. But Amy also knows that it can be frustrating to find a quilt at a garage sale or flea market and know absolutely nothing about its maker.

If the quilt top is in good shape, a quilt can be deconstructed by separating a worn backing—and the quilt label—from the quilt top. By writing her name inside, Amy makes sure that the quilt will still have a voice, even years down the road. Amy puts a lot of energy and pride into her quilty accomplishments. You never know what might happen to make that quilt top surface again, someday.

INNER DEMONS

Doubt	Rebuttal
You don't have the right kind of sewing machine.	As long as you have a walking foot that fits your sewing machine, you can quilt your quilt. Any machine will do.
Your sewing machine throat isn't big enough to fit the whole quilt in it.	That's fine, because the *whole* quilt doesn't have to be squished into the sewing machine throat. Typically, you only have to get half of the quilt in the throat to work from the center of the quilt out.
You don't have the right equipment.	You have a sewing machine. The extra equipment needed is a walking foot. Period. Everything else is optional.
You don't have time.	Find a way to enjoy the quilting part, and you will make the time.
You don't have the skills.	If you can sew a ¼-in. seam, you have the skills.
You'd rather be doing something else, like more piecing.	I hear ya! The closet will accept as many quilts as you can piece. But a quilt top won't keep anyone warm. And isn't that the point, really?
You can't. You can't. You can't.	You *can*, you *can*, you *can!*

Choose a Backing

If you're worried about quilting your quilt, an informed decision on the type of backing material can ease your concerns. Fussy prints on backing fabric hide lots of quilting sins. Plain or solid colors show off the quilting—which can be a good or bad thing.

Batting Up

The type of batting you choose enhances the quilt's purpose, but it can also direct the way the quilt is quilted. For more information about quilt batting, see pp. 31–32. A less confident quilter may not achieve the density of quilt stitches required for some types of batting. Steer clear of batting choices that require dense quilting, at least until you've gained some quilty confidence.

Hold the Mayo! Constructing the Perfect Sandwich

Puckers and pleats can appear mysteriously on the back of the quilt during the quilting process. How could that happen? It looks fine from the front of the quilt! It's really quite easy to avoid this sorry state of affairs, and it all comes down to one loaded piece of advice: Don't shortchange the steps needed to construct the quilt sandwich.

To make the quilt sandwich, make a run to the hardware store for some 2-in.-wide painter's tape. The blue stuff. Then, follow the steps below for foolproof quilt-sandwich construction!

1. Find a big, open space as large as your quilt backing. A bad choice would be the valuable antique wooden table that is reserved for special-occasion family gatherings. A good choice could be a hard-surface floor, like concrete or fabricated hardwood. Try to avoid a surface that might scratch easily.

2. Once the quilt backing is ready, following the steps on p. 74, lay the backing fabric on the hard surface, right side down.

3. Make sure the backing fabric is smooth and perfectly flat. Use several pieces of painter's tape—about 8-in. to 10-in. pieces—to secure the quilt backing to the floor (figure 1). Secure one side of the backing, then secure the opposite side, then the top and bottom. By the time you're done taping the backing to the hard surface, only little gaps along the sides—maybe 2 in. to 3 in. between tape strips—will not be secured.

FIGURE 1
Use painter's tape to secure all four sides of the quilt backing to a hard surface, like a concrete or fabricated hardwood floor.

4. As you place each piece of tape, use the tackiness of the tape to pull the backing gently toward the outer edge, to make sure it is taut. Readjust the tape as needed until you're satisfied. Consider this as the bottom slice of bread in your sandwich.

5. Place your batting of choice, roughly trimmed to size, on the backing. Don't worry about trimming it to the exact size just yet.

6. Smooth the batting perfectly even. Get in the middle of the quilt, if you can, and smooth the batting with your hands, working from the center outward. This is the middle of the quilt sandwich—the peanut butter and jelly, if you like.

7. Finally, lay the quilt top, right side up, on top of the batting without disturbing it. Working from the center out, smooth the quilt top so

it's perfectly even and bubble free. Make sure that at least 1 in. of batting is visible peeking out from underneath each quilt top edge.

8. Trim the batting all the way around the quilt so it's 1 in. away from the quilt top edge (figure 2).

FIGURE 2
The batting and quilt top are placed on top of the secured backing fabric. Smooth out any lumps or folds after adding each layer.

And that's the quilt sandwich! I'm hungry—I think I'll go make a ham sandwich before I start to baste the quilt. Mmm, basting! Make that a turkey sandwich!

Basting with Pins

With the quilt sandwich ready to baste, we're not quite out of the woods when it comes to preventing unsightly puckers and unintentional folds. A thorough pin-basting will achieve that end.

Basting Tools

You'll need some safety pins. I prefer curved safety pins, designed specifically for quilting, 1½ in. long. Plan on about 20 to 25 pins per square foot of the quilt.

To save your fingers, here's another specifically designed tool: a Kwik Klip™. The Kwik Klip has a hefty wooden handle like a rug-hooking tool and a blunt metal tip with grooves. If you are right-handed, hold the Kwik Klip in your left hand. With your right hand, insert the point of the safety pin in the quilt sandwich through all the layers. Travel about ¾ in., then use the Kwik Klip to hold the sandwich down while lifting the point of the pin through the sandwich so you can secure it. Lefties, switch hands.

1. If you can, place yourself right in the middle of the quilt with your container filled with safety pins.

2. Start anywhere. It's a myth that you have to baste from the center out. *Pin-baste*, that is. If you are thread basting, it's *critical* that you start from the middle of the quilt sandwich and work outward.

3. Insert one pin at a time, digging deeply enough with the pin to grab all three layers: the top, the batting, and the backing.

4. Continue to place pins, one at a time, every 2 in. or 3 in. If you make a fist and put it anywhere on the quilt, your hand should touch at least two pins.

5. While you are pin basting, consider the patterns in the quilt and contemplate potential quilting options. As you pin, develop your quilting strategy. Consider simple straight-line placement, or fancy it up with organic, free-form shapes.

6. Once the quilt is covered with pins, remove the tape holding the backing in place and fold the edge of the backing fabric to cover the edge of the quilt top. Then secure the folded fabric with another series of pins.

It's easy to get lost in the process of quilting your quilt. Without the last step, a corner of the backing fabric can flip under the quilt, in between the quilt and the sewing machine bed. If that happens, you'll need one more piece of equipment: a seam ripper.

OTHER BASTING OPTIONS

Pin basting a quilt that will be machine-quilted on a domestic sewing machine isn't the only option. You can also

• Spray-baste

• Use double-sided fusible batting

• Thread-baste

I prefer pin basting, especially for new quilters, for a few simple reasons: As you quilt, the pins leave a visible record of where the quilt is quilted. Conversely, it's easy to tell where the quilt *hasn't* been quilted. If the pins are gone, the quilt is quilted in those spots. If the pins are still there, the quilting isn't done yet. Plus, pins are reusable, and there's no overspray on the nearby surfaces or fusible material in the quilt sandwich.

Pin basting also slows me down and gives me one-on-one time with my quilt so she (the quilt) can tell me how she wants to be quilted. Before you discard that last statement as nutty, have you listened to your quilts lately?

Thread: What Color?

As discussed on p. 29, I prefer using cotton thread for all the steps in the quilt-making process. Thread color is another consideration.

Unfortunately, there aren't any color charts or must-do or must-not-do lists that make choosing the color of the quilting thread a no-brainer exercise. There are very few hard-and-fast rights and wrongs.

Still, consider these tips when choosing the quilting thread color for your quilt.

- Variegated threads tend to look best over solid fabrics. They can become a distracting now-you-see-it-now-you-don't element when used over multicolor sections of the quilt.

- In the quilt, light thread colors read cream, dark thread colors read black. Medium-range colors read closer to the thread color.

- No matter what the backing fabric looks like, choose the quilting thread color based on the quilt top, and match the bobbin thread to the top thread. Choosing matching top and bobbin thread will reduce the possibility for little dots of bobbin thread to peek up through to the top of the quilt. The slightest variation in tension can create the dots. If top and bobbin

thread match, the dots might be there, but you won't see them.

- Avoid using black thread for quilting. Against lighter fabric colors, it's very harsh. Against dark-colored fabrics, especially black, it's nearly impossible to see because the black color absorbs light. Instead of black, consider charcoal gray. The gray is less harsh but still provides a high contrast against lighter color fabrics, and it's visible on black.

- Unless you do a serious amount of thread painting, the quilting thread color will *not* correct piecing inconsistencies. So, don't get your hopes up that the upside-down half-square triangle unit will look right side up once you've done a little corrective quilting with some specially chosen thread colors.

Start Straight

The quilt is sandwiched and basted, a plan is in place, and the thread has been selected. We've put this off long enough; it's time to roll up the sleeves and dig in.

THE WALKING FOOT

The easiest starting point is straight-line quilting. A walking foot or a dual-feed foot is not all-important, but it's very helpful for straight-line quilting. Without it, the quilt sandwich might bunch up and create unattractive, poorly formed stitches. The walking foot applies forward-motion pressure from the top of the quilt to supplement the forward-motion pressure from the feed dogs, moving multiple layers of fabric under the needle at once.

You can quilt the entire quilt with straight lines or gently curved lines using the walking foot. If you're just starting out, experiment with straight-line quilting and get really comfortable with it before graduating to in-the-ditch quilting.

Be sure the fork-shaped arm on the walking foot is properly installed around the needle clamp.

IN-THE-DITCH QUILTING

In-the-ditch quilting is straight-line quilting that follows the seamlines. Each seam on the quilt has a downside. When the fabrics were pieced together, the seam allowance was pressed to one side, so one side of the seam sits higher on the quilt because of the two folded-under layers of seam allowance fabric. In-the-ditch quilting means that the quilting line follows the downside of the seam or the side of the seam without the seam allowances.

In-the-ditch quilting can be tricky—a little wobble of the quilt sandwich, and the stitching jumps to the upside of the seam, paired with a chunky-sounding *bump-bump-bump* instead of the usual *pfff-pfff-pfff* of the happy quilting stitch on the downside of the seam. With

TIP: When seams are pressed open, in-the-ditch quilting can sever the piecing threads. Proceed with caution and add additional straight-line or free-motion quilting nearby.

practice, the line of in-the-ditch quilting almost disappears in the puff of the quilt sandwich, creating a mysterious line of compressed texture in the quilt.

Most of my machine quilting begins with straight-line quilting to set the stage for the free-motion filler stitches. Often, my quilting strategy starts with in-the-ditch straight-line quilting around the border, then some more straight-line quilting around the blocks and sashing strips.

Remove the pins! Maybe I should have mentioned this earlier, but never sew over the safety pins. Needles break, the safety pins get sewn into the quilt by mistake—all kinds of bad things happen!

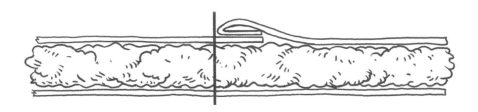

A cross section of the quilt sandwich, with the backing at the bottom, the quilt top with a seam at the top and the batting in the middle. The vertical line shows the ideal placement for stitch-in-the-ditch quilting— at the downside of the seam.

Make Your Knots Disappear

To start a line of quilting, drop the needle into the sandwich precisely where the quilting will start, then lift the needle without advancing forward. The needle will bring up a tiny loop of bobbin thread. Use a stiletto or the point of a seam ripper to grab the bobbin thread without ripping it (A). With the bobbin thread on top and with the thread tension released, pull the two thread ends until they are 3 in. or 4 in. long. Hold both threads with your finger as you start to sew (B). Make a few stitches, then let go and leave the thread on top of the quilt sandwich. If you see it, you won't inadvertently quilt over it.

Later, tie the thread ends in a square knot flush with the quilt. Pop the threads into a self-threading needle (C), and feed the point into the quilt right at the knot (D). Travel through the batting about 1 in., and cut the thread ends even with the quilt top.

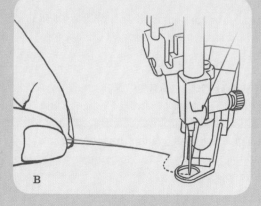

B

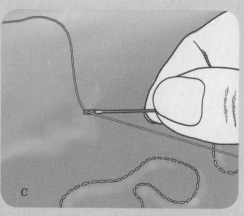

C

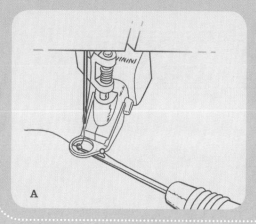

A

D

Check Tension

Every time you begin quilting a new quilt, it's an excellent idea to check the thread tension. Quilt about 5 in. or 6 in., then check the stitches on the bottom of the quilt. Are they nicely formed, like little miniature bumps of thread? Or is the thread just sitting there like a fishing line floating on a pond? Some sewing machines adjust for varying tension automatically, and some need to be adjusted manually. Don't forget to take a look at the stitches and adjust the upper thread tension accordingly. Look for more information on this subject on pp. 8–10.

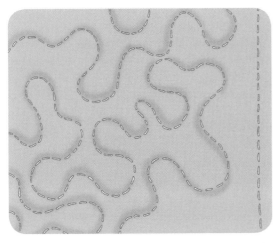

Well-formed, even stitches will look like little bumps of thread on the front and back of the quilt.

Move to Motion

My best advice to anyone who wants to graduate from straight-line quilting to free-motion quilting is to meander. Free-motion loops look a little like a road map filled with crazy, curvy twists and turns that never cross or intersect.

Big meander loops all over the quilt. Medium meander loops in the border. Medium-small meander loops in the sashing. Small meander or stipple loops in the block parts.

Practice meandering on one quilt. Then practice meandering on another quilt. Do it again on a third quilt. And a fourth one. And a fifth one. Meander until you can't bear to meander any more. Meander until you're really, really good at it. Then you are ready to try different kinds of free-motion patterns.

Why all the meandering? It's as simple as this: It's easy to do, but difficult to master. It's versatile, and when you get it, you *get* it, like hitting the baseball out of the park. When you've mastered the meander, the free-motion world opens up: loops, fans, back-and-forth corduroy lines that make you want to touch, and even feathers. The quilt is your canvas!

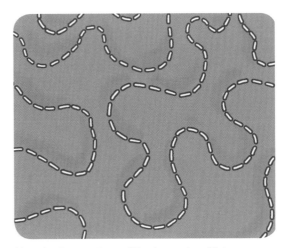

Meander free-motion quilting is a series of inter-connected, organic loops that don't intersect or cross, in a "perfect world."

Other Quilty Options

Machine quilting isn't for everyone. You've got choices and alternatives!

LONGARM TO THE RESCUE
You can send the quilt to your favorite longarm quilter. A longarm sewing machine is a specialized sewing machine with an extra-large throat that is set on a super-sized frame. The quilt is secured in the frame, and the sewing machine travels across the quilt for quilting.

ALL TIED UP
Tying is a classic, simple technique to secure the quilt layers. To tie a quilt, use yarn or heavy thread (like pearl cotton) to make the ties. The finished knots can be on the right or wrong side of the quilt, depending on your preference.

Thread an embroidery or chenille needle with the yarn or thread and insert it straight into the quilt from the side on which you want

> **TIP:** Be sure to check with your longarm specialist for any special instructions before presenting your quilt for quilting. Typically, a larger backing needs to be prepared. And some longarm quilters stock batting by the roll and prefer a specific brand.

the finished knots. Leave about a 2-in.-long tail. Take a small stitch and bring the thread back up through all the layers. Tie off in a square knot.

Ties should be no more than 3 in. to 4 in. apart across the quilt surface. After the tying is complete, clip all the thread tails to about $\frac{3}{4}$ in. long.

If you're not keen on all those loose threads on the front or back of the quilt from tying, you can use an embroidery stitch such as a colonial knot or, one of my favorites, a cross and twist stitch. The cross and twist stitch is especially nice for winter-themed quilts because the stitch looks like snowflakes or stars. Any of these stitches, as well as many other embroidery stitches in random or planned spacing, will do the trick to hold the quilt sandwich together. Travel from one stitch to the next through the batting. Keep in mind, when using embroidery stitches to quilt the quilt, the appearance at the top and bottom of the quilt may not match.

Tying a quilt is a particularly nice option to finish a quilt made from fabric that may stretch or bunch if subjected to the rigors involved in machine quilting. A T-shirt quilt like the one on p. 124 is a perfect example. Even with lots of pin basting, the stretchy T-shirt material can shift during free-motion quilting, and tying the quilt might create the best result.

Hand Quilting

We've all seen the images of quilters huddled around a large frame. But before you go all *Little House on the Prairie* on me, things are a little different now. Not that quilters—women and men—don't gather around the quilting frame to complete a quilt anymore, because they do. But quilting can just as easily be a solitary sport with a few different tools.

For starters, you don't need a sewing machine. I suppose that one is obvious. A few other tools you might consider include:

• A frame

• A sturdy hoop, 12 in. diameter or so

• Basting thread

• Quilting betweens, size 9, 10, or 11. Get a sampler pack of needles and use the one that feels best. I like betweens that have a bigger eye because quilting thread tends to be heavier weight. Speaking of thread . . .

• Quilting thread. Once again, I prefer 100 percent cotton that is coated to reduce the fuzz factor. Don't use coated cotton thread in the sewing machine.

• A sturdy, comfortable thimble, worn on the middle finger of your dominant hand.

The type of batting you select for a hand-quilted project could be different from what you use for machine quilting. A fluffy batting that is easy to needle through and doesn't have scrim is best. Lightweight polyester batting, 100 percent cotton batting, or wool batting can create a divine hand-quilting experience.

To baste a quilt for hand quilting, layer the backing, batting, and quilt top on a flat surface as you would when basting to machine-quilt,

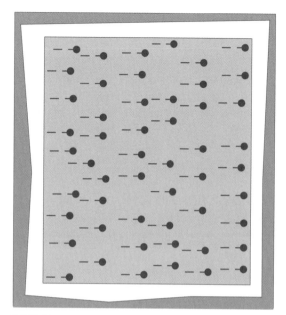

FIGURE 1
To prepare a quilt for hand quilting, layer the quilt sandwich, and working from the center out, secure the layers with straight pins, placed roughly in rows about 3 in. apart.

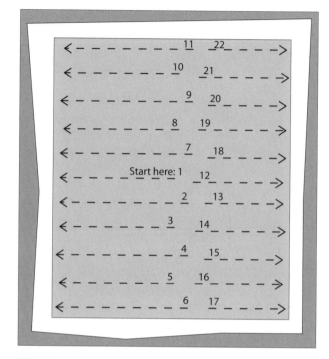

FIGURE 2
Work from the center of the quilt toward the edge with lines of long basting stitches. Remove the straight pins as the layers are secured with thread.

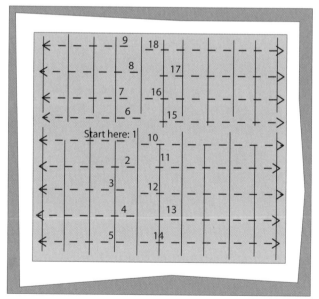

FIGURE 3
Rotate the quilt sandwich and complete thread basting with a second set of basting stitches at right angles to the existing threads.

but don't tape the backing to the surface. Starting from the center and working out, with straight pins, pin through all the layers in rows that are about 3 in. apart (figure 1).

Thread a needle, sharp size 9 or 10, with basting thread. Cut the thread about 24 in. long, and make a quilter's knot at the end (see p. 60). Insert the needle in the middle of the quilt and work outward in a straight line, forming big basting stitches through all the quilt layers (figure 2). Follow the numbered lines of stitching in sequence, and remove the straight pins as the quilt is basted. **Overlap the basting stitches in the center of the quilt. The illustration shows a gap for clarity.**

When you have about 3 in. or 4 in. of quilting thread remaining on the needle, make a backstitch—a short stitch on top of the last stitch.

Rotate the quilt 90 degrees and continue to baste in sequence, working from the center out (figure 3).

Hand-Quilting Best Practices

Here are a few tips from Pepper Cory, who's been hand quilting for 40 years and still loves it (peppercory.com):

"Hand quilters are a breed apart, and we love the slow and methodical process of hand stitching. But occasionally, a hand quilter begins to have problems. Hand quilting is a choice, and it ought to be enjoyed. When deadlines loom, it's easy to forget the time and spend hours quilting. The result can be neck and back fatigue, eyesight strain, and hand cramps.

- Using the right materials is critical. A bedsheet needles harder than yardage bought for the purpose, so why fight with the fabric? Plus, there are wide-back fabrics (90 in. or 108 in.) just perfect for backings.
- Needle knowledge. We might prefer different types, but I buy a "Made in England" needle. You can't beat English steel and nickel finishing. The needles bend less and stay sharp longer. Any needle that cuts your thread or doesn't glide easily between the layers of the quilt sandwich is not worthy of a hand quilter.
- If you quilt with a hoop, don't curl up in the recliner: The very best chair for hand quilting is a well-padded office chair. Good posture, not pretzeling up around your work, is critical when handling a hoop and quilt. Work at a table, with the hoop propped between your body and the table edge. The table surface supports the weight of the quilt, and the edge of the table provides a convenient angle for work.
- This brings us to lighting: The more the better! At a table, you can move a lamp around to illuminate your work.
- Take regular breaks—at least every 45 minutes—to stretch, move, and allow your eyes to focus on something besides the quilt.
- Last word of advice: Wear wrist cuffs. No matter how well-padded your physique, you have bony wrists. When wrists get cold, they are liable to ache. If you keep your wrists warm, your hands will be more supple, and you'll be able to hand-quilt longer and in more comfort."

The density of the basting stitches—how close the basting rows are to each other—depends on whether a frame, a hoop, or no hoop will be used while quilting. If a hoop will be used, the quilt sandwich should be basted at least 3 in. apart. For quilting without a hoop, the basting stitches should be closer together.

HAND-QUILTING TIPS

Whatever hoops or frames you elect to use, the key to success in the quilting stitch is 90 degrees in and 90 degrees out.

Start with about 36 in. of thread on the quilting between (or your needle of choice). Choose where you'd like to start—to avoid bunching and puckering, it's best to start in the middle of the quilt and work out. If you are using a hoop, hoop up the spot where you'll begin, and insert the needle into the top layer of the quilt nearby, but not at, your starting point. Travel through the batting and pull the needle up through the quilting start point. Note that we didn't put a knot at the end of the thread. Instead, roughly measure about half of the thread on the needle and leave the long end of the thread (the part without the needle) on top of the quilt. You'll come back to the other half of the thread later.

On the needle end of the thread, hold the needle with your dominant hand and stab the needle into the quilt through all layers so the needle is at a 90-degree angle to the quilt surface. Using your other hand, push the quilt sandwich up from the bottom, rotate the needle toward the hand below, then insert the needle up through all layers as close to a 90 degree angle as possible. Don't pull the needle through the quilt sandwich from top to bottom and back again. Throw away the concept of the stitching cards from childhood. Keep your dominant hand on top of the quilt and the "helper" hand underneath. Start with one stitch at a time. As you get more confident, load the needle with two or three stitches. Continue in this manner until you near the end of the thread.

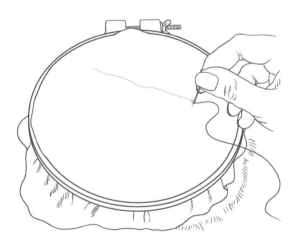

At the start of the line of quilting, insert the needle at a 90-degree angle.

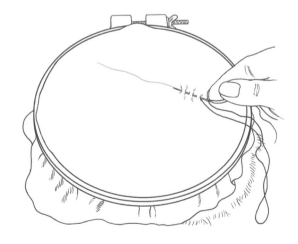

Using the "helper" hand underneath bring the needle back up through the quilt layers with the needle at a 90-degree angle to the fabric.

When you have about 3 in. or 4 in. of thread left, don't make a knot! Instead, feed the needle back and forth in the batting layer of the quilt sandwich four or five times between the existing quilting stitches, then snip the thread at the surface of the quilt top.

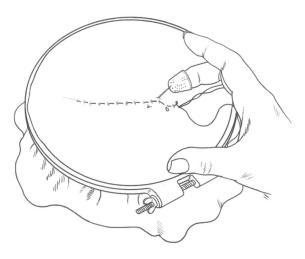

As you weave the thread end between the stitches, pivot the needle without pulling it completely through the quilt top, and continue weaving like a series of Ws. Be sure to use a metal thimble to push the pointy end of the needle back into the quilt sandwich.

Go back to the other half of the thread that was left on the quilt top, travel through the batting to the spot on the quilt where the quilting stitches began, and continue quilting.

HELPFUL MARKING TOOLS FOR HAND QUILTING

It's helpful to mark the quilt to follow your quilting plan easily. Paired with a straightedge or quilting stencil, the markings prepare the quilt for long quilting sessions. As with any marking tool, but particularly with those used on the front of the quilt, test the tool to make sure the markings can be removed. Quarter-inch tape, heat-erasable markers, chalk, and water-soluble markers are great tools. Air-erasable markers are also great—but know that you must quilt before the markings vanish or you will be sorely disappointed!

TIP: To form an even stitch, it's important to create a 90-degree angle between the needle and quilt backing from both sides. It's more important to have stitches that are equal in size and spacing on the front and back than it is to have tiny stitches that are un-evenly spaced or are uneven in size from front to back.

The Home Stretch: The Perfect Binding

The quilt is done, and the end is in sight. The backing and batting are trimmed, and the binding is cut and sewn end to end and pressed lengthwise wrong sides together to make one long binding strip.

The only thing left to tackle is binding the quilt! Except for those evil corners. Whether the corner of the quilt is a regular 90-degree angle or a different angle, the binding corners can be intimidating—but they don't need to be. To miter the binding at the corner, follow these steps:

- Leaving at least a 12-in. tail of binding to start, sew the binding to the first side of the quilt, raw edges aligned, (usually) ¼ in. away from the trimmed raw edge of the quilt.

- As you approach the corner, stop sewing with the needle in needle-down position about 6 in. from the corner.

- Make a mark on the binding at a 45-degree angle at the corner (figure 1).

- Return to sewing. When you reach the line, pivot and sew on the line, off the quilt. Place the corner of the quilt flat on the worktable. Fold the binding to the right, so that the raw edge of the binding and the raw edge of the quilt form a straight line (figure 2).

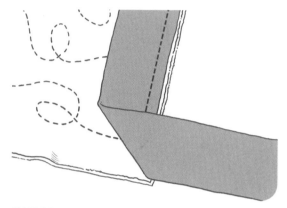

FIGURE 2
Fold the binding to the right so the raw edges of the quilt and the binding for a straight line.

- Then fold the binding back onto itself to the left so the quilt and binding raw edges are aligned. Pin the binding in place along the next side of the quilt (figure 3).

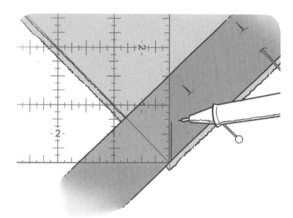

FIGURE 1
Make a mark at a 45-degree angle on the binding fabric directly above the trimmed corner of the quilt sandwich.

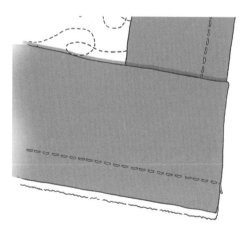

FIGURE 3
Fold the binding to the left onto itself, so the fold is aligned with the vertical raw edge of the quilt.

- Starting at the fold, continue to sew the binding onto the edge of the quilt as before. Complete the binding with a continuous binding closure, as described on p. 91. To hand-sew the folded edge of the binding, place the quilt on your lap with the backing facing up. Turn the folded edge of the binding from the front to the back and temporarily hold the binding in place with pins or clips. Slipstitch the binding fold to the quilt backing, traveling through the batting layer (figure 4). To keep the stitches invisible, insert the needle just behind the last stitch.

- To reduce bulk at the corners, as you approach the corner, park the needle and fold the right side of the binding over the left and secure with pins or clips (figures 5 and 6).

- Continue to slipstitch the binding onto the quilt, mitering each corner as you go.

This process is exactly the same with a corner that has an angle that is greater than 90 degrees.

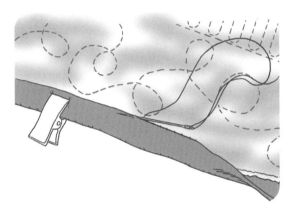

FIGURE 4
With the quilt on your lap, backing facing up, turn the folded edge of the binding to the back of the quilt and slipstitch the fold to the back of the quilt. Travel the needle through the batting later as you create the slipstitch.

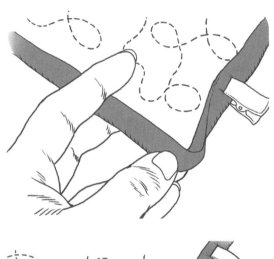

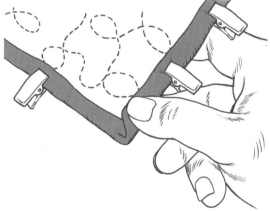

FIGURE 5 AND 6
To reduce bulk at the corner, fold the right side of the binding over the left, creating a miter at the corner. Folding right over left will evenly distribute the bulk at the corner front to back.

BIAS BINDINGS

A binding cut along the straight of the fabric grain may not work so well for a quilt with scalloped or curved edges. A stretchier binding is also a good idea when adding binding to a bag or anything with flexible edges. Some quilters feel that a bias binding on any quilt wears longer.

Making bias binding

When I first started quilting, I learned how to make bias binding from a square of fabric. You sew two seams, press the seams open, then cut yards and yards of bias binding. I probably used that method once or twice. Ick.

You might only have two seams to sew, but you start with a monster-size square of fabric and some pretty funky math to estimate how much binding you get, you end up with an odd-shaped, awkward tube to cut into binding strips, one layer at a time, the leftovers are weird shapes that don't fit into my tidy world of stash storage, and if you cut the square too big—I always did because after all the contortionist cutting I didn't want to start all over again—the leftover binding is enough for three king-size quilts! (Okay, I'm exaggerating a little.) Instead, I prefer to cut my strips from a rectangle of fabric.

- Start with the same quantity of fabric as if you were to use width-of-grain strips. Square up the sides of the rectangle and remove both selvages at a 90-degree angle to the sides.

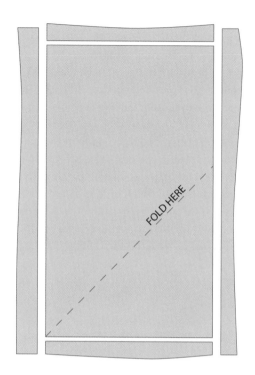

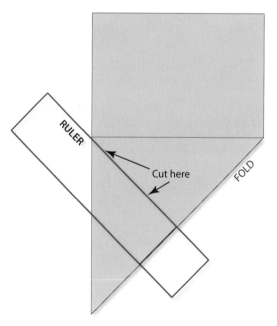

- Fold the corner of the quilt on the diagonal as shown. Place a ruler on the fabric with a horizontal line aligned with the fold.

- Make the first cut from fold to corner. Cut strips 2¼ in. wide (or your preferred binding width) until the rectangle is used up. Fold the fabric parallel to the first fold if the fabric gets too long for the ruler you're using. Connect the strips end to end. Most of the strip ends are at a 45-degree angle; some will need a fresh bias cut. Be sure to offset the angled strips to accommodate the seam allowance as you sew the strips end to end.

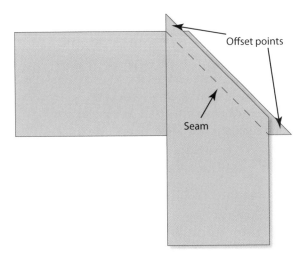

Offset points

Seam

- Press the connecting seams open, then press the binding lengthwise with wrong sides together, and attach the binding to the quilt as shown on pp. 86–87.

Different Finishing Options

Pillowcase turn is a popular, super-easy way to finish a small quilt without making a binding.

Layer the batting, then the backing right side up, then the quilt top centered on the backing right side down. Pin around the perimeter of the quilt. To keep the layers from shifting during sewing, add a few straight pins in the center.

With a walking foot, sew ¼ in. away from the edge of the quilt top, removing the pins around the edge as you sew. Leave an opening big enough to turn the quilt inside out, usually about 10 in. on a small quilt. Remove the pins in the center of the quilt, then turn the quilt right side out through the opening. Hand-stitch the opening closed. Pin-baste and quilt as desired.

TIP: To keep from sewing all the way around the quilt and forgetting to leave an opening for turning, place two pins at the stopping point to remind you to stop there.

A Hurry-Up Binding

To make a faux binding on a turned quilt, complete the quilt top and add a small border in a coordinating solid color; borders that are cut 1½ in. wide or less work best. As described on p. 89, layer, stitch, and turn the quilt, pillowcase-style, and close the opening. Stitch-in-the-ditch at the last border seam, then quilt the rest of the quilt as desired. The poofy edge will look just like binding, without the extra fabric or stitching!

The Quilt's Voice

You finish a quilt. Yay! And it goes off into the world. Yay! And it doesn't have a label. Uh-oh!

Years from now, how will anyone remember who made it, and whether it has traveled far or stayed close to home? What pattern was used? How old is the quilt? What type of batting is inside? How shall it be washed? In the excitement of finishing a quilt, it's easy to overlook that one last important step: the label.

Use some leftover fabrics from the quilt top to make a simple label. With a permanent fabric marker, print the quilt's story on the label and turn under the edges of the label fabric, then slipstitch the label to a corner of the quilt on the back. Dress it up with embroidery, cross-stitching, or detailed piecing. Keep it simple or make it fancy; just do it.

WHAT TO INCLUDE ON A QUILT LABEL

- The name of the quilt or the title of the piece

- The quilt maker's name

- Who quilted it

- In what city was it made

- Was the quilt made for a special occasion? Add some information about the occasion and for whom the quilt was made.

- The date the quilt was finished and the date of the special occasion

- The kind of batting inside

- Any special washing instructions

- The source of the pattern: Is it an original design or from a book or pattern?

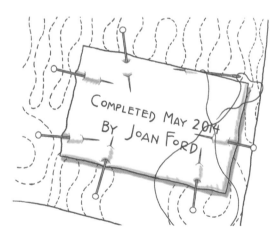

A quilt label is usually attached to the back of the quilt with a slipstitch.

Continuous Binding Closure

After trimming the batting and backing even with the quilt top, start along one edge and sew the binding to the quilt edges, leaving about 24 in. of the binding unsewn: 12 in. at the beginning and 12 in. at the end. Place the unbound section of the quilt flat on your work table. Lay the binding ends evenly along the raw edge of the quilt and fold the binding back on itself so the folds meet.

Make two marks on the top binding layer one-half the width of the binding from the fold. (I usually cut my binding strips 2¼ in., so half of that is 1⅛ in.) Make two lines on the binding, each 1⅛ in. away from the fold. This calculation works for any width double-fold binding.

Fold the quilt onto itself, and pin the quilt layers, creating some slack to allow you to work easily with the binding ends.

Bring the binding end from the left above the quilt, onto the work table and open the fold. Place the binding rightside up so you can see the marking line. Open the crease, and fold the right binding end, wrong sides together, at the marking line. Align the fold from the right binding with the edge of the left binding. At the same time, align the marking on the left binding with the edge of the right binding.

Open the right binding fold, and draw a line parallel to the quilt top, from edge to edge. Secure the binding with pins on both sides of the drawn line. Sew on the line. Trim about ¼ in. away from the seam (unpin the quilt to test it first, if you like). Pin and sew the remaining binding to the quilt edge. There—you've got an almost continuous binding!

Caring for
Your Quilt

You might think that once you've finished constructing your quilt, you'd be done worrying about all of those *bad things* that could happen. But life doesn't like to keep things simple! Here's some advice to counteract anything that life throws at you—and your precious quilt!

Oopsie

It's easy enough to fix a piecing mistake before the quilt is sandwiched and quilted (see p. 50), but what about finding a mistake after the quilt is sandwiched, quilted, and bound?

I suppose one option is take the stance that no one is perfect and that the quilt is simply playing out its role in reminding you of your humanity. Seriously, take a step back and ask yourself, how bad is it? Will you be the only one who ever notices the mistake?

If the problem creates a persistent reminder, perhaps the best way to fix a quilted quilt is by creating an appliqué correction. There are two potential options—the "disguise" or the "cover-up." In either case, create an appliqué shape and slipstitch or machine-stitch it in place.

To "disguise" the offending area, re-create a shape from the focus print, or choose a common appliqué shape like a heart, a flower, or a leaf large enough to mask the error. Apply fusible web to the back of the appliqué, fuse the shape onto the quilt, and blanket-stitch the appliqué edge through all the layers. You may want to repeat the appliqué in one or more places on the quilt to balance the design.

The "cover-up" is all about re-creating the pieced section. Make a section with the correction, turn the seam allowance under with an iron, and position the corrected pieced element over the error and slipstitch the turned edges to secure the shape. A few quilting stitches may be in order to match the quilting patterns in neighboring sections.

These fixes really don't make the problem go away. The bottom line is: What's the better story?

Storage

Now that your quilt is completely done, it's time to enjoy it. And when you aren't enjoying it, it needs to be stored.

The best way to store a quilt is flat on a bed. The second-best way to store a quilt is dropped haphazardly in a clump so it doesn't have planned folds that the quilt might "remember" over time.

I suppose both of these methods of quilt storage are rather unreasonable in most households. Most people don't have a spare room just for quilts. A prolific quilt maker can quickly turn that bed in the guest room to a real-life version of "The Princess and the Pea." Or, imagine walking from room to room avoiding little piles-o-quilt randomly scattered along one hallway or another. Most folks need to resort to folding their quilts to store them.

> **TIP:** Resist the urge to fold a finished quilt right sides together. That puts stress on the piecing and appliqué crunched together at the folds. Fold the quilt so the right side is on the outside of the fold. Cushion the fold with archival paper that has been crumpled up to support the entire length of the fold.

The Dog Ate My Quilt!

Barbara made a lovely queen-size quilt. She carefully collected the fabrics, assembled the quilt top, and quilted it. A beauty, to be sure. It was a gift for her son.

Fast-forward to the day Barbara got a call from her son. "Mom, do you know how to repair a quilt?" Reilly, the pet golden retriever, had chewed a hole in the quilt where it was folded. So it really wasn't just one hole, it was a more complicated repair. Barbara appliquéd matching fabric to cover the holes on the front. From the back, she inserted new batting and patched up the backing.

To make sure her son would have a reminder of what happened, Barbara found some paw-print fabric, made one of the patches for the back in the shape of a dog bone, and appliquéd it in place. Speaking of pets and quilts . . .

Pat and her cat were hanging out in her sewing room. Pat was busy cutting lots and lots of diamonds for her next quilt project. As she cut, Pat placed her carefully cut shapes in a plastic storage container. Stacks of them. She was just about ready to start sewing when the cat stepped over to the box and vomited in it. Some problems you can't, and shouldn't, fix.

WHAT SHOULD YOU DO TO MAKE YOUR QUILT FORGET THE FOLDS?

Some types of batting—cotton or cotton/poly blend, in particular—can leave unappealing scrunch marks where the quilt has been folded, and the fold marks can be difficult to remove. If you find that a favorite quilt has been folded and has an unsightly wrinkle that won't go away, these steps have helped me relax the wrinkle on a quilt or two:

• Lay the quilt flat, with the undesirable fold sandwiched between two clean, damp bath towels.

• Let the soggy sandwich sit for about 20 minutes.

• In the dryer, tumble-dry the quilt and towels on a low setting.

• Remove the quilt and towels from the dryer just before they are completely dry and lay the quilt flat to finish drying.

• Repeat if the fold marks persist.

Splish-Splash! Washing Tips for Your Quilt

It can be really daunting when a quilt gets dirty. What's the best way to get it clean? This process can achieve some pretty fantastic results:

- Wash the quilt in cold water on a gentle cycle.

- If this is the quilt's first washing, include a dye-catching sheet in the washing machine with the quilt, even if you don't suspect the fabrics might run. Better to be safe than sorry.

- Remove the quilt from the dryer before it is completely dry and lay it flat to finish drying.

- Never wash a quilt that has raw edges exposed. If you must wash an unbound quilt, stabilize the raw edges first with a zigzag stitch sewn around the entire quilt perimeter.

- A rag quilt, or a quilt that includes raw-edge appliqué, is an exception to the last item. Be sure to thoroughly clean the dryer's lint-catching screens after washing raw-edge-style quilts.

- Bleach will almost always leave an unappealing result. Don't go there.

 ## Give the Quilt a Breather

At least once a year, open up the quilt, shake it out, and lay it flat. Refold it a different way. Avoid folding right down the center or in the same place each time. I try to fold my quilts in uneven thirds. Also avoid the following:

- Long-term storage in plastic bags or wrapped around uncovered plastic tubes. Plastic is an oil-based product, which can damage the quilt over time.
- Direct sunlight, to avoid fading colors.
- Prolonged exposure to moisture, or the risk of mildew increases.
- From time to time, it's necessary to store your quilt in plastic. If you must put the quilt in a plastic bag, don't store your quilt, even temporarily, in a dark opaque plastic trash bag. If you stick to see-through plastic bags, anyone in the household—including those whose weekly chores include taking the trash to the curb—will be unlikely to make an unfortunate mistake.

STAINS

Removing a stain from a quilt is just like removing a stain from any other fabric—with, perhaps, a few extra precautions.

The key to removing a stain from your quilt is knowing what kind of stain it is. Food? Blood? Ink? Once you know the composition of the stain, follow the steps below in order.

- Step away from the quilt.

- Cry.

- Curse or scream.

- Calm down and continue breathing.

Note: Repeat the above four steps as many times as necessary before proceeding. It's imperative to remove stains from a quilt with a level head. Hasty action could cause permanent, irreversible damage.

- Approach the stain as you would any other problem—one step at a time.

- Remove as much of the staining material as possible before it dries. Do not apply heat with an iron or in the dryer until the stain has been completely removed, or you risk setting the stain in the fabric permanently.

- Do some online research to determine what remedies work best to remove the type of stain you're dealing with. An online search using key words such as *stain*, *quilt*, *save me*, *I'm desperate* can be very helpful.

- Blot, don't rub.

- Consider testing a remedy on a part of the quilt that isn't visible. For example, hydrogen peroxide may remove bloodstains nicely, but it may fade darker colors. (If you're concerned about that, try another remedy first.)

- Place a clean cloth or paper towel underneath the stain while you apply the remedy. The cloth will accept the stain as the remedy pushes the stain off the quilt fabric. Replace with a clean cloth frequently.

- Avoid using bleach at all cost. In the most desperate moment, it will be a tempting option. Don't do it. Just don't.

Perhaps the best piece of advice for removing a serious stain from your quilt is to have patience and perseverance. The sad, honest truth is that some stains, particularly stubborn, set-in stains, are here to stay.

Bleeding dye

When I was preparing to write this book, I put a message out to my online followers, asking them to tell me about things that went wrong with their quilts. The problem that turned up the most frequently was fabrics that ran after the finished quilt was washed. Among sad stories of ruined quilts, I found a few hopeful suggestions to remove bleeding dye:

Laurie: I read somewhere if you soak the quilt in Wisk® detergent, the stains come out. It works great!

Janet: I made a small paper-pieced quilt for a quilt show and auction. I added a red border that must have been a hand-dyed fabric. I needed to steam the quilt to remove some of the quilt markings and, you guessed it, it bled. I put Synthrapol in the sink with water, and let the quilt soak. The quilt was saved; it went on display in a show, won a ribbon, and was sold!

The Case of the Bloody Quilt

The quilt was coming along beautifully—hand-pieced hexagons, several years in the making—and I was in the process of quilting it, by hand, of course. Then something caught my peripheral vision. A bloodstain. A bad one. About an inch in diameter on cream-colored prints. My breathing stopped. My eyes popped wide open. And the only question that came to mind was "where did this come from?" I had no idea how the stain got there, but there it was.

By the time I noticed it, the stain was perfectly dry. I resisted the urge to apply water and cleaners and chemicals, and took the quilt to my wash room.

The spot was in pieced fabric, near the edge of the quilt. I removed enough basting to see if the batting was also stained (it wasn't). I folded up a few sheets of white paper towel and slipped them in between the stained fabric and the batting, then turned on the cold water. I sprayed a few drops of a laundry presoak detergent directly on the stain, then applied cold water with a few squishy dabs from a clean sponge, and walked away.

When I returned five minutes later, I could see that it was working. But the stain was still there. I blotted the stain with the damp sponge from the top, and replaced the paper towel inside the sandwich with a fresh one. I was happy to see that the stain was transferring to the inside towel nicely. I repeated the process a few times more. Cold water, laundry presoak solution, apply pressure with a squishy sponge. It worked. The stain cleaned up beautifully and dried without a trace.

Mo: My sister embroidered some beautiful redwork angels on quilt blocks using a thread she hadn't used before. She turned the stitched pieces over to me, and I added some piecing and quilting. I popped the piece in my wash basin to soak with some mild soap and walked away. When I came back, the block was pink, with beautifully stitched red angels! The cure? Denture-cleaning tablets. They worked! It may have lightened the red thread a bit, but it's barely noticeable.

Morna: I finally finished a quilt for my nephew. It started as a baby quilt, but he's now 10, so the quilt had to be upsized. I used some wonderful blue batik fabric for the backing and binding. With the quilt complete, I washed the quilt, but when I removed it from the wash, I discovered that the dye from that perfect blue batik backing had run onto the front of the quilt—not all over, but enough to leave me crushed. I washed the quilt again with a dye-trapping sheet. And again. And again. I think I went through half a box of those sheets before the unwanted dye finally came out. End of the story: My nephew loves his quilt!

Use It!

As much as I feel it's important to take this advice, and take care of your quilts, I feel even more strongly that it's important to *use* your quilts. Yes, they will get stains on them, and eventually they'll show signs of wear. A weak spot in the fabric will tear, appliqué pieces will loosen, and pieces will fall off. It's going to happen. And it's all a part of the life cycle of a quilt.

Sometimes the quilt gets so much use that it can get to the point that it can't be repaired any longer. Or maybe the quilt has never been used. For example, I have a queen-size quilt that I will never finish. It's halfway quilted, and I simply don't like the project anymore. If some parts of the quilt are salvageable, why not take those parts and make something new, like Candy's camera case, described at right. If it's going to get worn out, then wear it out to its fullest, and enjoy every last thread!

Armed with gobs and gobs of how-to advice, stories, and practical solutions, consider yourself prepared to take the reins and go! The projects that follow offer a varied sampling of quilty techniques to try.

Candy's Camera Case

I met Candy at a local quilt shop in the southern tier of New York State. She leads a variety of quilting workshops and events there. Here's her story of transforming an imperfect quilt into another perfect project.

"Many years ago, I made an octagonal table topper, and I loved it! It was a gorgeous red and green fabric with metallic gold through it, and it was my first attempt at machine quilting. But hey, what could go wrong with a little table topper? In my mind, this was the perfect way to ease into machine quilting.

"Well, when I finished, it laid flat in the red center, but the green borders looked like the ruffle on a clown suit!

"I tucked it away until after Christmas. I received a digital camera as a gift, and I wanted to make a padded case for it—and there was that table topper! I cut it in half, made some tucks and folds, added some Velcro®, and voila: I had a lovely camera case!

"Now, what to do with the other half of the table topper?"

Apply Yourself: Four Projects Waiting for a Quilter

These four patterns will give you the opportunity to apply all of the skills and information that we've covered in this book. Make one project, make them all, but whatever you do, make sure that you make them your own! And don't forget to visit www.taunton.com/GoodQuilters to download your bonus project, the Seeing Stars Quilt.

The Miter Touch Quilt

Sometimes, I hear frustration from quilters when I mention mitered borders: *They are so difficult!* In fact, I think they are easier than traditionally pieced borders. All you need is a little practice and an easily executed technique. For this project, start with two somewhat coordinated large-scale prints, cut them up, then add mitered borders to each one. Next, piece them together to create a quilty collage of "pretty." I chose two similar large-scale floral prints, and paired them with four solid fabrics to complement the floral prints. To keep things simple, all the border strips from each fabric are cut the same size.

FINISHED SIZE
- 48 in. by 60 in.

FABRICS
Note: Directional prints are not recommended.
- 1 yd. dark gray large-scale print
- 1¼ yd. light gray large-scale print
- 1 yd. pink
- ⅔ yd. light taupe
- ⅔ yd. natural
- ⅓ yd. pale yellow
- ½ yd. binding
- 3¼ yd. backing, seamed horizontally
- 52-in. by 64-in. batting

ADDITIONAL SUPPLIES
- Fabric marking pen

CUTTING

It's a good idea to keep the fabric pieces organized as you cut and prepare to sew. Make nine little "kits" for each mini quilt top by stacking, pinning, and labeling each large-scale fabric piece along with its associated borders. Sew each mini quilt top start to finish and set it aside. Once all the mini quilt tops are complete, arrange and assemble the quilt almost like a puzzle.

To keep your pieces organized, the borders and large-scale print fabrics are identified by number or letter throughout the pattern instructions and illustrations. Letters are used for the dark gray sections and numbers for the light gray sections. Refer to the illustration on p. 108.

What to Do when Your Ruler Isn't Big Enough?

I like to use a ruler that is 6½ in. by 12½ in. Several of the fabrics in this project are bigger than my ruler. If you find yourself in a similar situation, here are some strategies to cut the "biggies."

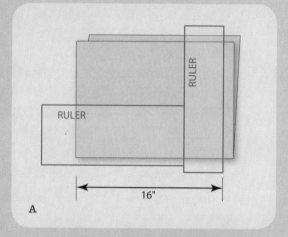

A

- Pair 'em up. Let's say you need to cut a 16-in. strip, but you only have two rulers handy: a 6½-in. by 12½-in. ruler and a 4½-in. by 12½-in. ruler. Place one of the 12½-in. rulers horizontally, then place the remaining ruler vertically. You might have to do a little math to trim the strip to the correct length, but if you add 12½ in. to either 4½ in. or 6½ in., you get a measurement that's greater than 16 in. (A)

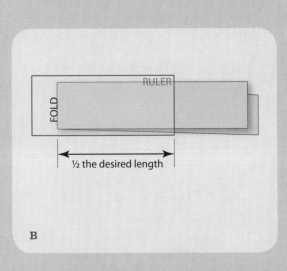

RULER

FOLD

½ the desired length

B

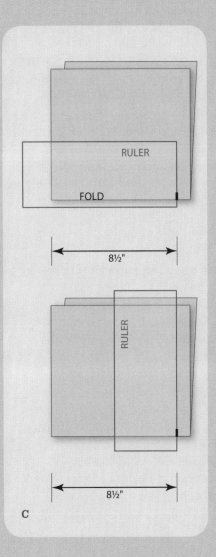

RULER

FOLD

8½"

RULER

8½"

C

- Divide and conquer. Fold a fabric strip in half, then use the ruler you have to measure one-half the distance from the fold to make your cut. (B)

- A nick in time saves nine. If your ruler is 6½ in. wide, but you want to cut a strip that is 8½ in. wide, lay the ruler so the long side follows the fold of the fabric. Measure the 8½ in., and make a little nick in the fabric with your rotary blade. Without moving the blade, rotate the ruler so the short end is parallel to the fold and a horizontal ruler line is aligned with the fabric fold, then use the long edge of the ruler to make the cut. (C)

DARK GRAY LARGE-SCALE PRINT

Cut one 16-in. width-of-fabric strip, then cut one 16-in. by 19-in. rectangle (A) and one 11½-in. by 13-in. rectangle (C).

Cut one 7½-in. width-of-fabric strip, then cut one 7½-in. by 16½-in. rectangle (B) and one 6½-in. by 7½-in. rectangle (D).

LIGHT GRAY LARGE-SCALE PRINT

Cut one 12-in. width-of-fabric strip, then cut one 12-in. by 24-in. rectangle (1) and one 11½-in. by 17½-in. rectangle (2).

Cut one 8½-in. width-of-fabric strip, then cut one 8½-in. by 10-in. rectangle (5).

Cut one 7-in. width-of-fabric strip, then cut one 7-in. by 22-in. rectangle (3) and one 5½-in. by 15½-in. rectangle (4).

PINK

- Cut ten 2½-in. by 42-in. strips, then from these strips cut *two* each of the following dimensions.
- 28 in. (A-sides), 25 in. (A-top/bottom)
- 30 in. (1-sides), 18 in. (1-top/bottom)
- 24 in. (2-sides), 18 in. (2-top/bottom)
- 22 in. (4-sides), 12 in. (4-top/bottom)

LIGHT TAUPE

- Cut nine 2-in. by 42-in. strips, then from these strips cut *two* each of the following dimensions.
- 22 in. (B-sides), 13 in. (B-top/bottom)
- 36 in. (1-sides), 24 in. (1-top/bottom)
- 12 in. (3-sides), 27 in. (3-top/bottom)
- 16 in. (5-sides), 18 in. (5-top/bottom)

NATURAL

- Cut twelve 1¾-in. by 42-in. strips, then from these strips cut *two* each of the following dimensions.
- 24 in. (A-sides), 21 in. (A-top/bottom)
- 16 in. (C-sides), 18 in. (C-top/bottom)
- 33 in. (1-sides), 21 in. (1-top/bottom)

- 15 in. (3-sides), 30 in. (3-top/bottom)
- 13 in. (5-sides), 15 in. (5-top/bottom)

PALE YELLOW

- Cut six 1½-in. by 42-in. strips, then from these strips cut *two* each of the following dimensions.
- 30 in. (A-sides), 27 in. (A-top/bottom)
- 24 in. (B-sides), 15 in. (B-top/bottom)
- 11 in. (D-sides), 12 in. (D-top/bottom)

> **Tip:** For this quilt, the border lengths have been provided, so you only have to cut the strips, organize them by section of the quilt, and sew them together in sequence—short/medium/long for each side of the quilt sequence.

HOW TO DETERMINE THE BORDER LENGTH

Let's say you want to substitute traditionally pieced borders with a mitered border on any quilt. A mitered border always requires more fabric than a traditionally pieced border.

Let's use print A for an example. Let's assume the center rectangle is a quilt all by itself. To determine the length of each border, you need to know the dimensions of the center and the width(s) of the border or borders.

Starting with the side borders, begin with the top-to-bottom dimension of the quilt top. In our example, the large-scale print is 19 in. long. The first side border will finish to 1¼ in.

Notice that we're mixing unfinished sizes with finished sizes. I start with the unfinished quilt top dimensions, then continue on through the process with the finished sizes.

Back to the border width: Start with the 19-in. top-to-bottom border. Multiply the finished width of the first border (1¼ in.) by two (2½ in.). Add the two results, then add a little bit more. For a small quilt like this, 2 in. is "little bit" enough. For a larger border, add 3 in. or 4 in. Then round up. In our example, add 19 in. plus 2½ in. plus 2 in., then round up—you'll get 24 in. The first side border is cut 1¾ in. wide by 24 in. long.

For the second side border, start again with the top-to-bottom dimension of the quilt top (19 in.) then progressively add twice the width of the first border (1¼ in. x 2 = 2½ in.) and twice the width of the second border (2 in. x 2 = 4 in.) plus a little extra (2 in.), then round up (28 in.).

Finally, to calculate the length of the third border, start with the unfinished top-to-bottom dimension of the quilt top (19 in.), plus twice the width of the first border (1¼ in. x 2 = 2½ in.), plus twice the width of the second border

(2 in. x 2 = 4 in.), and twice the width of the third border (2 in.), plus a little extra (2 in.), and round up (30 in.). You'll need two of each border, one for each side of the quilt.

Repeat the whole process for the top and bottom border dimensions, starting with the unfinished side-to-side dimension of the quilt top, or 16 in. in the example.

THE MITER STEPS

1. To make a border strip set for each side and the top and bottom of the quilt, center and sew one, two, three, or more border strips of each length in sequence (inner border, middle border, outer border or, short, middle, and long). Make a total of four border strip sets.

2. Press the seams on two opposite borders toward the inner border.

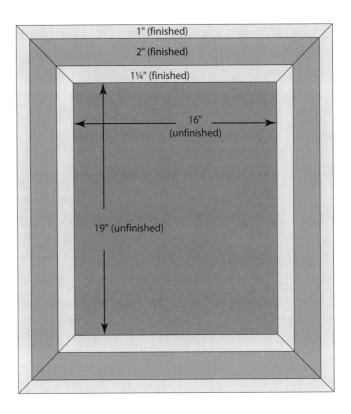

FIGURE 1

FIGURE 2

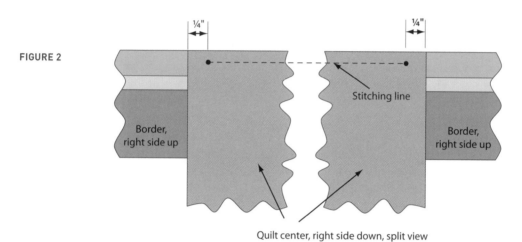

¼"   ¼"

Stitching line

Border,
right side up

Border,
right side up

Quilt center, right side down, split view

Draw sewing line
between end of seam
and edge of border
along the ruler.

RULER

Border seam

FIGURE 3

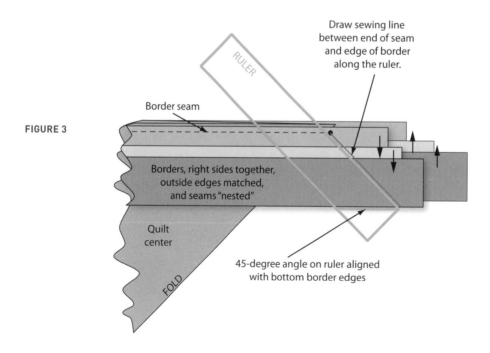

Borders, right sides together,
outside edges matched,
and seams "nested"

Quilt
center

FOLD

45-degree angle on ruler aligned
with bottom border edges

3. Press the seams on the remaining two opposite borders toward the outer border (figure 1).

4. Center and sew the side borders and the top and bottom borders to the quilt, starting and stopping ¼ in. from each edge of the quilt top (figure 2).

5. Choose one of the corners to miter. At the selected corner, fold the quilt top in half diagonally, wrong sides together, and at the same time, place the outside borders, right sides together, so both the top and bottom edges of the border form a straight line. Lay the quilt, particularly the border end, flat on a work surface, as shown (figure 3).

6. Place a straight ruler with a 45-degree line on top of the folded quilt. Place the 45-degree line even with the borders' outside edges and the straightedge of the ruler just intersecting the very end of the border seam.

7. Draw a line with a pencil or quilt marking tool from the end of the border seam to the edge of the border along the edge o the ruler.

8. Secure with pins along the drawn line.

9. Carefully transfer the quilt to the sewing machine and sew directly on the drawn line, starting at the border seam intersection and sewing outward toward the quilt edge.

10. Return the quilt to the worktable and trim the excess border fabric, leaving a ¼-in. seam allowance to the outside of the mitered seam.

11. Repeat the mitered corner steps for the remaining three corners.

12. When all corners have been sewn, press from the back, pressing the mitered seam open and the quilt/border seams toward the border. Then press the entire border assembly from the front.

ASSEMBLE

ADD BORDERS TO EACH FLORAL PRINT

Working one section or "mini-quilt" at a time, and following the steps on pp. 105–107, add mitered borders to each floral print rectangle. Sew any multiple borders together first, then add the borders to their corresponding large-scale prints.

The unfinished dimensions for each mini-quilt, after the borders are sewn, are

A: 24½ in. by 27½ in.
B: 12½ in. by 21½ in.
C: 14 in. by 15½ in.
D: 8½ in. by 9½ in.
1: 21½ in. by 33½ in.
2: 15½ in. by 21½ in.
3: 12½ in. by 27½ in.
4: 9½ in. by 19½ in.
5: 14 in. by 15½ in.

FIGURE 4

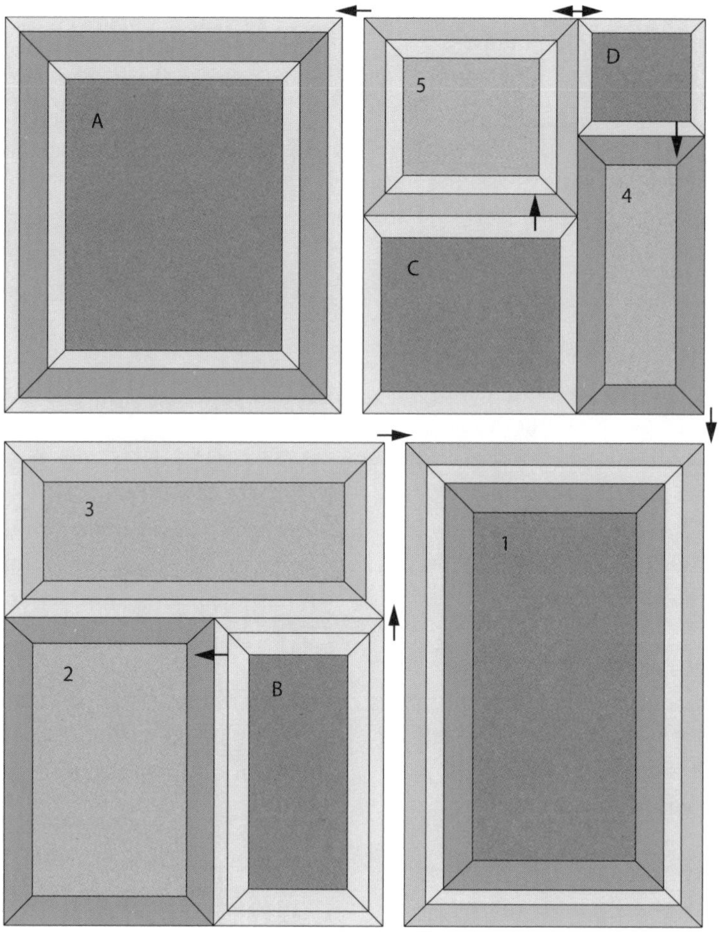

Arrange the sections as shown (figure 4).

To construct the upper section of the quilt top, sew C to 5, then sew 4 to D. Press the seams as indicated on the illustration. Then sew 5/C to D/4. Press the seam in either direction. Then sew 5/C/D/4 to A to complete the top section of the quilt top.

To construct the lower section of the quilt top, sew B to 2, then sew 3 to 2/B, then sew 1 to 3/2/B. Press seams as indicated after each addition. Sew the upper and lower sections to each other to complete the 48½-in. by 60½-in. quilt top.

QUILT AND BIND

Layer the backing, the batting, and the quilt top; baste. Quilt as desired. Cut six 2¼-in. width-of-fabric strips for the binding. Sew the binding strips together, end to end, using a diagonal seam. Press the seams open, then press the binding in half lengthwise, wrong sides together.

Trim the batting and backing even with the quilt top. With the raw edges aligned, sew the binding to the front of the quilt using a ¼-in. seam. Miter the binding at the corners. Turn the folded edge of the binding to the back of the quilt, and hand-stitch in place.

Sweet Tweet Table Runner

The center piecing for this table runner may be completed by hand or machine. Because the simple shapes intersect in a labyrinth of Y-seams, I feel this project seems better suited for hand stitching. Review the steps and illustrations outlined in Sharon Stroud's comments on pp. 57–59, and assemble the quilt center one seam at a time. Two appliqué options are available to make the table runner ends. The branch and flower arrangement is a good start if you've never done appliqué before. Those looking for more challenge will find the option with the bird a bit more complicated—particularly the branches and bird details.

Note: To hand-piece the quilt center, review the steps outlined on pp. 57–59. The pattern instructions assume that you are hand-piecing the quilt center.

FINISHED SIZE
- 14 in. by 46 in.

FABRICS
- Six fat quarters (18 in. by 21 in.), in coordinated colors for piecing and appliqué
- ½ yd. neutral solid for piecing and borders
- ¾ yd. backing
- 15-in. by 48-in. batting
- ⅓ yd. binding

ADDITIONAL SUPPLIES

- Needles, for hand sewing: size 9, 10, or 11
- Piecing thread, snips, scissors
- Pencil or fabric-marking tool
- Template plastic, freezer paper, or card stock to make hand-pieced templates
- Sewing machine, to add the borders and binding
- Hand-quilting thread or pearl cotton for the quilting
- Needles for quilting: betweens for quilting cotton or embroidery needles for pearl cotton

CUTTING AND FABRIC PREPARATION

One of the benefits of hand quilting techniques is that, for the most part, you can step away from the cutting mat and make smaller cuts with scissors, a rotary cutter, and a smaller cutting mat. It's not for everyone, but a change of scenery can be nice!

FAT QUARTERS

From each fat quarter, cut one 6-in. by 21-in. strip and reserve it for the appliqué shapes. From the remainder of each fat quarter, prepare as many as eight hexagons (figure 1) and as many as five half-hexagons (figure 2) for hand piecing—for a total of forty-eight hexagons and twenty-six half hexagons. Draw the seamline using freezer paper or template plastic for the template, then cut the shapes, adding a ¼-in. seam allowance on each side as you cut. Note that the shapes provided are the finished size, without seam allowances.

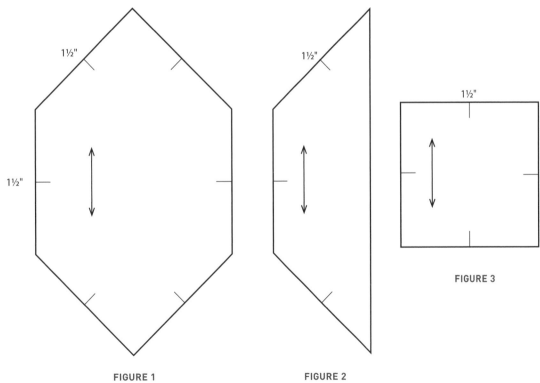

1½"

1½"

FIGURE 1

1½"

FIGURE 2

1½"

FIGURE 3

NEUTRAL SOLID

Cut two 1½-in. by 42-in. strips.

Cut one 6½-in. by width-of-fabric strip, then cut the strip in half to make two 6½-in. by approximately 20-in. rectangles. These will be trimmed to 5½ in. by 14 in. after the appliqué shapes have been applied.

From the remainder of the fabric, prepare 30 squares (figure 3 on p. 111) for hand piecing—draw the seamline using freezer paper or template plastic for the template, then cut the shapes, adding a ¼-in. seam allowance on each side as you cut. Note that the shapes provided are the finished size, without seam allowances.

(figure 3 on p. 111)

TIP: For illustration purposes, when the fabric pieces are arranged right side up, you wouldn't see the drawn seam allowance lines on the wrong side of the fabric. They are shown here so you can see more clearly where the seams will be.

PREPARE TABLE RUNNER CENTER

Arrange the first row and a half of half-hexagon and hexagon shapes, right side up on your worktable.

Start with the two corner pieces, place them right sides together, match the seam marked by the number 1 on the illustration below, and pin at the end points and match-marks. Knot the thread, then sew by hand with a small running stitch from point to point, starting with a backstitch and ending with a double backstitch. Snip thread (figure 4).

Replace the sewn half-hexagons into the arrangement. Pick up a sewn half-hexagon and the neutral square immediately to its left. Place the square right sides together with the half-hexagon, with the edges indicated by the number 2 aligned as shown, and the pieced half-hexagon in front (figure 5). Match and pin the end points and match-marks. Knot the thread, then sew by hand to the seam intersection, and backstitch.

Pass the needle through the seam intersection directly at the corner point, and park the needle temporarily without breaking the thread.

Pivot the square into position for seam number 3, then match, pin, and sew the seam. Begin with a backstitch, end with a double backstitch, then snip the thread. Remember to backstitch every time the needle is "loaded" and pulled through (figure 5).

FIGURE 4

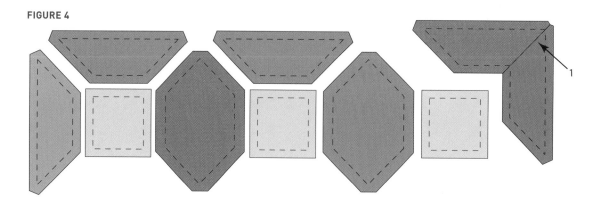

Continue to sew one piece at a time across the row. Replace the sewn parts in the arrangement before picking up the next piece to sew in place. Pass through seam allowances, and double backstitch and break the thread when you can't go farther. Follow the sequence shown. Sew seams 4 and 5, and break the thread. Then sew 6. Next, sew 7 and 8, then 9 and 10. Sew 11 by itself. Then sew 12 and 13, and finally 14 and 15 (figure 5).

While right-handed sewists will work right to left, left-handed sewists will work left to right.

When you complete the row, add the next row as shown. Technically, you can sew all the way across this row, adding one hexagon shape at a time, without breaking the thread. However, to avoid knotting, fraying, and thread breakage, don't start with more than 12 in. to 18 in. of thread on the needle. Double backstitch when

you "reach the end of your rope," and start a new thread with a quilter's knot (figure 6).

Continue to add one row at a time to the arrangement, and sew one piece at a time to the quilt center. Where the four 90-degree corners intersect, be sure to pass through all three seam intersections before adding the next piece of fabric. Draw up the thread firmly to make a crisp point where the points meet.

When complete, press the seams from the back as described on p. 45. Since you've sewn point to point, not edge to edge, all the seam intersections will furl. The quilt center is approximately 11½ in. by 37 in.

Measure the quilt top before trimming the side borders. Trim each 1½-in. by 42-in. neutral side border to 1½ in. by 37 in. Sew a border to each side of the quilt by machine. Press the seam toward the border. Set aside (figure 7 on p. 114).

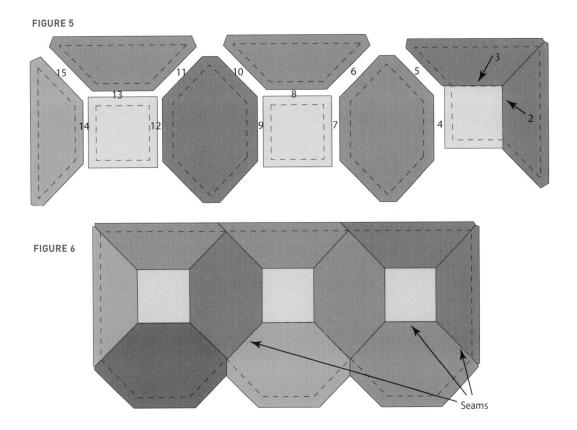

FIGURE 5

FIGURE 6

Seams

FIGURE 7

1½" x 37"

APPLIQUÉ

Using the 6-in. by 21-in. fat quarter pieces, trace the appliqué motif (on p. 116) centered on the wrong side of the 6½-in. by 20-in. neutral solid fabric. The motifs are shown in reverse.

Secure the appliqué shapes to the background. For the back-basting appliqué method, add the numbered shapes to the background fabric in sequence—sew all the 1s first, then the 2s, and so on.

Use the darkest of the fabrics for the branches, choose a bird-friendly print for the bird motif, and use the remaining four fat quarter pieces for the flowers. Make two appliqué panels. Trim each panel to 5½ in. by 14 in. Be sure to measure the quilt top before trimming the appliqué border (figure 8).

Sew an appliqué border to each end of the quilt, then press the seam toward the border.

TIP: Choose hand or machine appliqué as detailed on pp. 50–57, select your preferred method, and review the steps. This pattern has two different appliqué arrangements. Because of the smaller pieces, the motif with the bird on the branch is more difficult than the branch with flowers only. If this is your first attempt at appliqué, choose the branch with flowers alone. Or omit the appliqué altogether and replace the appliqué panel with a plain fabric strip.

QUILT AND BIND

Cut the backing fabric in half along the fabric fold to make two 20-in. by 27-in. pieces. Sew the backing rectangles together along the 20-in. side, then press the seam open. The backing is approximately 20 in. by 54 in.

Layer the backing, batting, and the quilt top; baste. Quilt as desired. For additional hand-quilting details, review the steps on pp. 81–85.

Cut four 2¼-in. width-of-fabric strips for the binding. Sew the binding strips together by machine, end to end, using a diagonal seam (see pp. 88–89). Press the connecting seams open, then press the binding in half lengthwise, wrong sides together.

Trim the batting and backing even with the quilt top. With the raw edges aligned, sew the binding by machine to the front of the quilt using a ¼-in. seam. Miter the binding at the corners. Turn the folded edge of the binding to the back of the quilt, and hand-stitch in place.

TIP: Once the appliqué has been secured by hand, press the appliqué panel. Always press appliqué from the back. Before pressing, place a clean piece of terry cloth (such as a towel) on the ironing board, then place the completed panel right side down on the terry cloth and press.

FIGURE 8

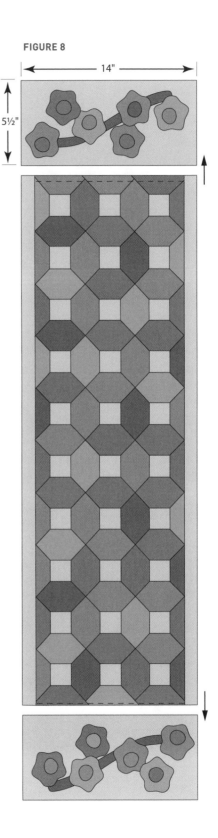

14"

5½"

Enlarge templates by 200%

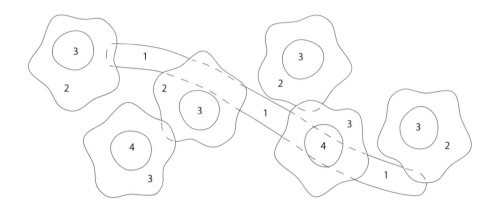

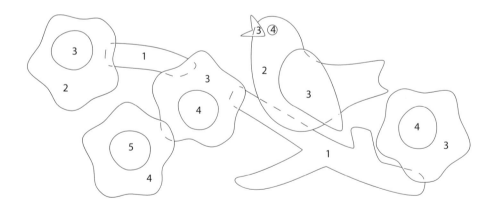

Panel Panache Quilt

A panel is a single illustration or an arrangement of several smaller illustrations on fabric. Some quilters call them "cheater panels." Panel sizes can vary, but they are usually printed on ⅔ yd. of fabric, or 24 in. by 42 in. A panel can be made into a quilt all by itself—just add backing, batting, and a bit of quilting. For me, the resulting quilt is a bit small. Slapping on a border or two is a good option, but sometimes it's fun to experiment with a different technique. This project offers a fun and funky pieced border treatment that can turn virtually any size panel, along with a few specially chosen stash fabrics, into a modern-inspired lap quilt or wall hanging.

FINISHED SIZE
40 in. by 52 in., varies

FABRICS
- One preprinted panel, approximately 24 in. by 42 in.
- Ten ¼-yd. by width-of-fabric strips for the border prints. Select a variety of prints in colors that progress from light to dark or from one color to a second color.
- ¼ yd. black or neutral solid for faux binding
- 2 yd. backing, seamed horizontally
- 45-in. by 60-in. batting

ADDITIONAL SUPPLIES
- Pearl cotton for tying option
- Embroidery needles

CUTTING

Trim the panel to approximately 24 in. by 40 in. Exact measurements are not critical. Block the panel as described on p. 34 before trimming, if necessary.

BORDER PRINTS

Arrange the ¼-yd. fabric pieces so they transition from the darkest value of one color, to lighter and lighter values of that color, then to light, medium, and dark values of the second color. While keeping the fabrics in value and color sequence, cut the following strips:

- 8½ in. by 42 in.
- 3½ in. by 42 in.
- 5½ in. by 42 in.
- 6½ in. by 42 in.
- 4½ in. by 42 in.
- 3½ in. by 42 in.
- 6½ in. by 42 in.
- 4½ in. by 42 in.
- 5½ in. by 42 in.
- 8½ in. by 42 in.

FAUX BINDING

Cut six 1¼-in. by 42-in. strips.

MAKE THE PIECED BORDERS

Strip-piece the border fabrics in sequence. Press the seams in one direction. The pieced panel is approximately 42 in. by 52½ in.

Cross-cut the pieced panel into four 2½-in. by 52½-in. strips for the inner borders, four 1½-in. by 52½-in. strips for the middle borders, and four 5½-in. by 52½-in. strips for the outer borders. Fold the pieced panel to cut across the strips as you would fold yardage to cut strips as described on pp. 33–34 (figure 1 on p. 120).

ATTACH THE BORDERS

Arrange the inner border on each long side of the quilt, so similar colors are on opposite corners. Measure and trim the border. Secure each border to the sides of the panel, and sew. Press the seams toward the panel (figure 2).

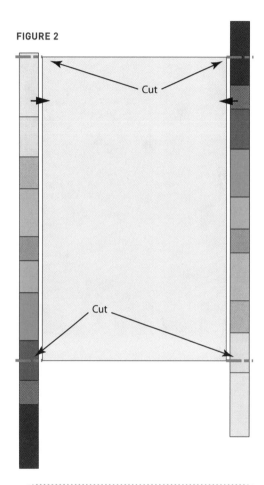

FIGURE 2

Cut

Cut

TIP: This project is a great use for stash fabric! The border elements can be a whack of this and a strip of that, ranging from 3½-in. to 9-in. width-of-fabric strips.

FIGURE 1

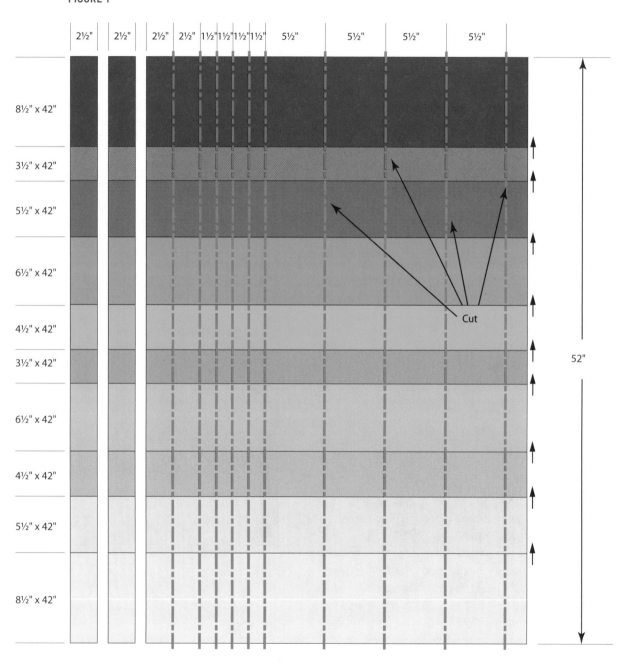

Arrange the inner borders on the top and bottom of the quilt, so matching colors are on opposite corners, as shown. Roughly center each border in a pleasing arrangement, then measure and trim the border as before. Secure the borders with pins, and sew. Press the seams toward the panel (figure 3).

Similarly, arrange the middle borders on the sides of the quilt, so the color arrangement is opposite of the inner border. To decide on exact placement of the border fabrics, slide the pieced border along the quilt edge to identify a pleasing arrangement, then measure, trim, and sew the middle border to the sides, top, and bottom of the quilt. Press the seams toward the border after each addition. Repeat the process with the top and bottom middle borders.

Finally, arrange the outer borders on the sides of the quilt, arranging the colors to match the inner border. Slide the border to identify the most pleasing arrangement of the pieces. Measure, trim, sew, and press toward the border. Add the top and bottom borders in the same way (figure 4 on p. 122).

FIGURE 3

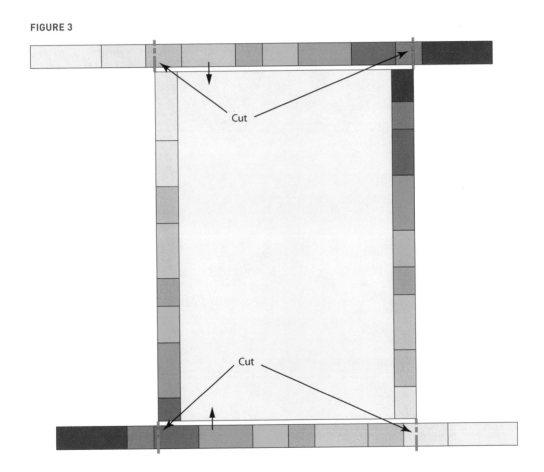

FINISHING

Sew three 1¼-in. by 42-in. strips end to end using a diagonal seam. Press the seam open. Cut the strip in half to make two 1¼-in. by approximately 60-in. strips. Repeat to make a total of four strips for the faux binding.

Measure, trim, and sew the side faux binding strips to the quilt top. Press the seam toward the border. Measure, trim, and sew the remaining two faux binding strips to the top and bottom of the quilt top. Press the seams toward the borders (figure 4).

Layer the batting and backing, right side up, and the quilt top right side down, then pin to secure all layers as described on p. 89 for a pillowcase finish. Leave an opening about 10 in. wide on one side of the quilt. Trim the batting and backing even with the quilt top. Remove all pins, then turn the quilt right side out. Sew the opening closed by hand with a ladder stitch. Quilt as desired.

FIGURE 4

What if my panel is a different size?

With some simple math, this pattern is easily adaptable to a panel that is a different size. For a different example, I cut a 15-in. by 24-in. section off a larger panel for the quilt center.

To determine the length of the pieced border panel, start with the longer dimension of the quilt center—in my case, 24 in. is the top-to-bottom dimension. Add the finished width of the first two borders, or 3 in. times *two* (6 in.), then add 10 percent to that sum.

24 + 6 = 30 + 3 (10% of 30) = 33

Next, start with the shorter panel dimension, or 15 in. from side to side. Add the sum of all three borders (finished width): 2 + 1 + 5 = 8 in. Multiply by two to get 16. Then add 10 percent.

15 + 16 = 32 + 3 (10% of 32) = 35

Use the larger of the two results, or 35. That's how long the sum of the border strips needs to be. I found eight fabrics that I wanted to use for the border from my stash. You can use as few as 6 or as many as 10 or 12 for a larger panel. It's up to you.

Since this panel is smaller than the original panel, I didn't want any one strip to be wider than 6 in., nor less than 2 in.—there's no magic formula for that, only my preference. Because I used eight fabrics, I randomly selected eight numbers between two and six to become my cut strip widths. Before I cut my strips, I added up the numbers. If the total was less than 35 in., I added 1 in. to an individual strip width, or deducted 1 in. from one or more measurements if the total was more than 35 in. Remember to work in finished sizes, then add the ½ in. for seam allowances before you cut.

In the end, I cut my strips 5½ in., 4½ in., 5½ in., 2½ in., 6½ in., 5½ in., 3½ in., and

6½ in. The total is (40 in. if you include all of the ½ in. seam allowances)—close enough to the 35-in. goal! I then cut my strips in sequence, strip-pieced the strips to make the border, added the panel, and cut the border strips, four each of 2½ in., 1½ in., and 5½ in. wide, following the original pattern. The key to the success of making this project in a different size is sewing the first border to the longer sides of the panel, regardless of how the panel print is oriented.

Since this smaller version of Panel Panache is more suitable for a wall hanging, I omitted the faux border and layered the backing, batting, and quilt top, then basted the quilt sandwich, quilted it, and bound it with four 2¼-in. by 42-in. binding strips. The mini-version of the quilt finished to about 31 in. by 40 in. For more details on attaching the binding to the quilt, see the instructions on pp. 86–87.

Warm Memories T-Shirt Quilt

After carefully selecting one-of-a-kind T-shirts from a cherished collection, it's easy for a quilt newbie to stop short before the first cut is made. Let's face it, once the T-shirt is cut, it's not a favorite T-shirt anymore. *No pressure there!* Add in variables like stretchy knit material and interfacing, and the intimidation factor can be a deal breaker!

You can follow Andrea's advice (see the sidebar on p. 133) and skip the interfacing altogether, then tie the quilt to avoid the challenge of quilting over the stretchy T-shirt knits, or you can take the middle road and stabilize the stretchy T-shirt material with single-sided fusible batting instead of using nonwoven interfacing. The batting will be softer, the knit T-shirt material will be stabilized beautifully without adding lots of stiffness, and the unruly, rolly edges of the T-shirts will be kept in check inside the quilt sandwich. Plus, the quilt will be much easier to quilt by machine because of the stabilizing effect of the fused batting. The added pieced elements and appliqué dots use T-shirt parts such as sleeves and backs that are often overlooked.

FINISHED SIZE
- 48 in. by 60 in.

FABRICS
- 12 medium to extra-large cotton T-shirts, washed without fabric softener or dryer sheets

- 3 yd. backing, seamed horizontally
- 2/3 yd. binding

ADDITIONAL SUPPLIES
- Single-sided fusible batting
- 12½-in. square ruler or larger for trimming T-shirt motifs

- Walking foot
- Permanent fabric marker
- ZigZapps!™ Circles by Quiltsmart®, two panels of 12 circles each (optional), or plain fusible interfacing

CUTTING

BATTING

- Cut six 12-in. squares.
- Cut six 8-in. squares.
- Cut six 4-in. by 12-in. rectangles.
- Cut six 4-in. by 8-in. rectangles.
- Cut four 6½-in. squares.
- Cut twenty-eight 6-in. by 6½-in. rectangles.

PREPARE T-SHIRTS

Deconstruct by cutting each T-shirt along one side and around the sleeve. Cut across each shoulder seam, through the collar, and around the sleeve seams. Reserve the sleeve materials for the appliqué dots.

Select six T-shirts for the larger blocks and six T-shirts for the smaller blocks. Open a deconstructed T-shirt that has been selected

TIP: While no special equipment is needed, a walking foot or even feed option on the sewing machine is recommended for the quilt top construction. To keep thread from shredding, proceed slowly and increase the stitch length while piecing the T-shirt quilt top.

for the larger block, and place it flat, but not stretched, on the cutting mat, paying particular attention to the printed motif. Fussy-cut the motif from the T-shirt so that it is 13 in. square.

Repeat with all 12 T-shirt motifs. Six large motifs are cut 13 in. square, and 6 are cut 9 in. square. Set each motif aside carefully, without stretching it. The edges may curl slightly.

From the remaining T-shirt material, cut a matching set of 5-in. by 9-in. and 5-in. by 13-in. rectangles. Make a total of six sets of rectangles. Set each rectangle aside for the pieced blocks. For the pieced border, cut thirty-two 7-in. squares. Reserve the remaining T-shirt material for the circle details.

Note that instead of the usual ¼-in. seam allowance, I've added an additional ¼ in. to each side of the cut T-shirt dimensions. Because the T-shirt material rolls and stretches, the extra fabric makes the stretchy T-shirt pieces a little easier to work with. Since the T-shirt material is soft, the added bulk in the quilt sandwich shouldn't be a concern.

FUSE THE BATTING TO THE CUT-UP T-SHIRT

Place a 13-in. T-shirt square right side down on the ironing board. Flatten, but do not stretch the material. Center a 12-in. square of fusible batting on the T-shirt fabric. To avoid getting fusible glue on the iron, be sure to place the fusible side of the batting facedown against the wrong side of the T-shirt material. Then fuse with a hot iron, adding several puffs of steam from the iron to activate the fusible glue.

Repeat to fuse each 13-in. square, 9-in. square, 5-in. by 13-in. rectangle, and 5-in. by 9-in. rectangle to its coordinating batting piece, which is 1 in. smaller on each side (figure 1).

Select four 7-in. T-shirt squares for the corners and fuse a 6½-in. batting square to the wrong side of the T-shirt material so two edges of the batting and T-shirt fabric are aligned. Fuse the remaining twenty-eight 6-in. by 6½-in. batting rectangles to the remaining 7-in. T-shirt squares so one edge of the batting is aligned with the T-shirt fabric edge as shown (figure 2).

The blocks in the quilt center will be sewn on all four sides; keeping the batting out of the seam allowance will reduce bulk. At the quilt's edge, one side of the 7-in. T-shirt square—two sides at the corners—will be the edge of the quilt. Even though the binding will cover the raw edge of the quilt, having the batting fused all the way to the edge will keep the quilt from having a deflated channel along the binding.

FIGURE 1

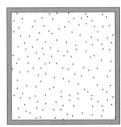

13" T-shirt square with
12" batting square.
Make 6.

9" T-shirt square with
8" batting square.
Make 6.

5" x 9" T-shirt rectangle with
4" x 8" batting rectangle.
Make 6.

5" x 13" T-shirt rectangle with
4" x 12" batting rectangle.
Make 6.

FIGURE 2

7" T-shirt square with
6½" batting square.
Make 4.

7" T-shirt square with
6" x 6½" batting square.
Make 28.

CONSTRUCT THE QUILT CENTER

Arrange the 13-in. and 9-in. square blocks into four rows of three blocks as shown, alternating larger and smaller T-shirt squares. Next, arrange the 5-in. by 9-in. and 5-in. by 13-in. rectangles with the 9-in. squares, keeping matched rectangle colors together [figure 3].

Note: In the illustration, the dotted lines represent the batting edges. Since the quilt pieces are arranged right side up, the batting is not visible.

Working one pieced block at a time, place the 9-in. square right sides together with the 5-in. by 9-in. rectangle, so the batting edges are aligned. Note that the T-shirt fabric edge may not align exactly. Use your fingers to feel the thickness, hold the fabric pieces up to a light, or use pins to make sure the batting edges are aligned, particularly at the corners. Pin to secure all the layers along the seam before sewing.

Using a walking foot or even feed option, and without sewing through the batting, sew the T-shirt material directly along the right edge of the batting [figure 4]. Cut the thread, and finger-press the seam in either direction [figure 5].

FIGURE 3

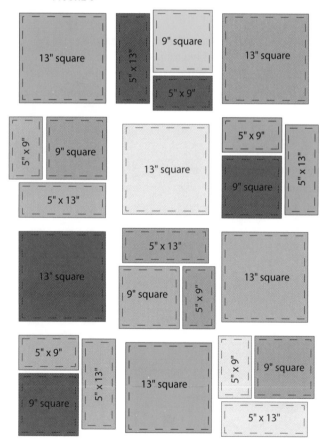

FIGURE 4

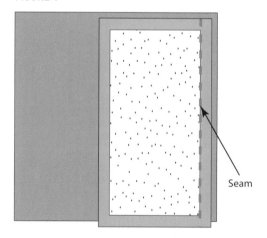

FIGURE 5

Similarly, sew the 5-in. by 13-in. rectangle to the side of the pieced unit (figure 6). Finger-press the seam toward the 5-in. by 13-in. rectangle. The pieced block will be 13 in. square based on the T-shirt fabric, or 12 in. square based on the batting. Note that placement of the pieced block elements vary for each block.

Remember to replace the pieced elements back into the quilt arrangement after each step because the T-shirt motifs will very likely be directional. By returning the pieces to the arrangement, you will avoid problems later with blocks that are accidentally rotated to one side or the other, or upside down.

FIGURE 6

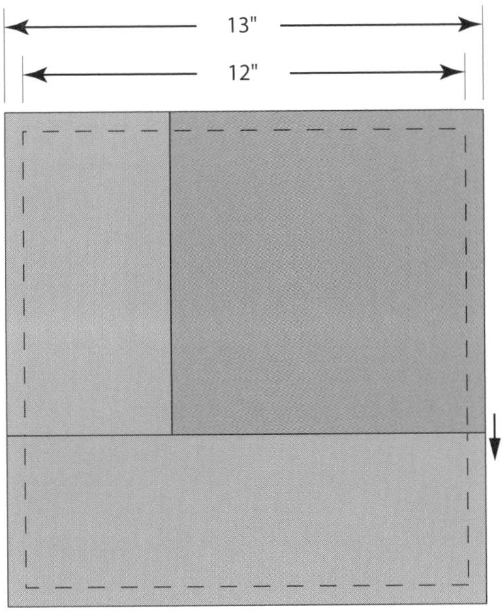

13"

12"

Upsize Me!

There are four different configurations of the pieced block in this quilt, identified by the placement of the 9-in. square. As you follow the diagonal placement of the pieced blocks from upper left to lower right, the 9-in. square alternates from upper right to lower right as your eye travels from block to block.

Simultaneously, the 5-in. by 13-in. rectangle alternates from side to side along the diagonal, then from top to bottom in the next diagonal. The placement of the 5-in. by 13-in. rectangle is notable, because the decorative T-shirt dots are always sewn onto the longer rectangle, starting at the end of the rectangle closest to the 9-in. square.

If you want to upsize this quilt, keep the alternating pieced-block configuration in mind as you begin to lay out the design.

Repeat to make all six of the pieced blocks. For each step, remember to align the batting edges, sew just off the batting edge, press the seam allowance to one side, and replace the block into the quilt arrangement after each addition and before proceeding to the next step. Before sewing the blocks into rows, add the circle appliqué detail to each pieced block.

MAKE CIRCLE APPLIQUÉ

Using a permanent fabric marker, trace 10 of the 3½-in.-diameter circles and six each of the 3-in.- and 2½-in.-diameter circles onto the smooth side of the fusible interfacing, leaving about ½ in. between the shapes.

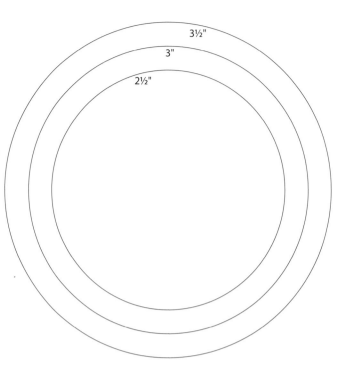

FIGURE 7

TIP: Why not make the pieced blocks before laying out the quilt? When constructing a quilt that includes pieced blocks and blocks made from a single fabric, typically pieced blocks are made first, and then arranged into rows with the single-fabric blocks. In this case, the pieced block construction depends on its placement in the quilt. By arranging the quilt first, then constructing the pieced blocks after their positions in the quilt has been identified, you have a preview of the finished project, including color placement.

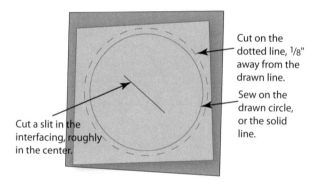

Cut a slit in the interfacing, roughly in the center.

Cut on the dotted line, 1/8" away from the drawn line.

Sew on the drawn circle, or the solid line.

Rough-cut the shapes at least ¼ in. away from the drawn lines. Fold each interfacing circle in half, and make a cut in the center about 1 in. long. You'll use the cut for turning later.

From the T-shirt scraps and sleeve material, rough-cut 30 "chunks" of fabric, each about 4 in. square. Mix up the colors, and make the combinations playful.

Place each interfacing circle on a plain T-shirt scrap that has been rough-cut to size.

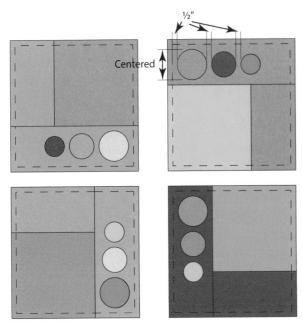

FIGURE 8

Make sure the fusible side of the interfacing is facing the right side of the T-shirt material. Pin the interfacing onto the T-shirt material without stretching the T-shirt scrap. Using a walking foot, sew on the drawn line. Trim the T-shirt material and interfacing about ⅛ in. to ¼ in. away from the sewn line (figure 7).

Turn the shape right side out through the opening in the interfacing. Retrieve a pieced block from the quilt block layout, and arrange three circles in the larger rectangle (figure 8). Place the 3½-in.-diameter circle ½ in. away from the rectangle batting edge (which will also be about 1 in. away from the edge of the T-shirt rectangle), then place the 3-in.-diameter circle ½ in. away from the 3½-in. circle, and place the 2½-in. circle ½ in. away from the 3-in. circle as shown. Each circle is centered across the 4-in. batting width (figure 8).

Fuse the circles onto the pieced block with a hot iron and a puff of steam. Using a walking foot or dual feed option, secure around the edge of the appliqué circle with a blanket or zigzag stitch. Repeat for all six pieced blocks.

¾-in. seam?

All this talk about ¼-in. seams, and now I have to sew the binding ¾ in. away from the edge of the quilt—what's up with that?

The extra-wide binding makes a playful finishing statement on this quilt, which is filled with big chunks of color. To sew the extra-wide binding seam, look for an L-shaped guide in your sewing machine tool kit. Check the sewing machine manual to review how to install the guide on your walking foot—usually it's just a matter of loosening a screw, inserting the guide in a hole in the body of the walking foot, then tightening the screw again. Make sure the guide arm is ¾ in. away from the needle position. As you sew, watch that the guide follows the trimmed edge of the quilt.

If you don't have a guide in your gadget bag, or if you can't figure out how to use it, measure ¾ in. to the right of the needle position with a small acrylic ruler. Place an acrylic adhesive strip or a short stack of three or four sticky notes on the sewing machine bed to make a guide for the fabric edge.

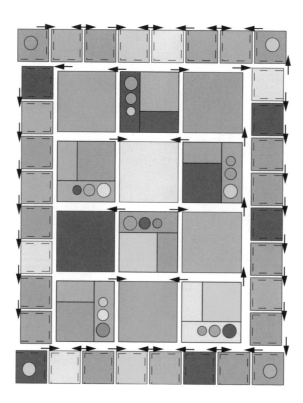

FIGURE 9

COMPLETE THE QUILT CENTER
Sew the blocks into four rows of three blocks each. With the blocks right sides together, continue to align the batting edges, not the T-shirt edge, and sew along the batting edge. Press the block seams in alternate directions by row, as shown. Then sew the rows together. Press the row seams in one direction (figure 9).

ADD THE BORDER
Center one 3½-in. circle appliqué on each of the four 7-in. corner squares, fuse, and secure with a blanket or zigzag stitch, as with the blocks.

Arrange the 7-in. squares around the quilt center. Use eight squares for each side border and six squares for the top and bottom border. Using the batting as a sewing reference point, sew the squares together to make the borders. Add the corner squares to each end of the top and bottom borders. Press the seams (figure 9).

Sew the borders to the quilt, sides first, then top and bottom. Press the seams toward the border after each addition.

QUILT AND BIND
Layer the backing and the quilt top. Since the batting is already fused onto the quilt top, you don't need to layer batting in between the quilt top and the backing. Baste, then quilt as desired. T-shirt material is stretchy, proceed carefully and distribute bulky spots as you quilt.

Cut six 3½-in. by 42-in. strips for the binding. Sew the binding strips together end to end using a diagonal seam. Press the connecting seams open, and then press the binding in half lengthwise with the wrong sides together.

Trim the backing even with the quilt top. With the raw edges aligned, sew the binding to the front of the quilt, using a ¾-in. seam. Miter the binding at the corners. Turn the folded edge of the binding to the back of the quilt, and hand-stitch it in place.

T-Shirt Quilt Tips from a Pro

T-shirt quilts aren't all that difficult to make, but a few things can go terribly wrong if you aren't careful. It boils down to one teeny-weeny issue: T-shirt material is knitted, and, therefore, it's very stretchy compared to woven quilting fabrics. Andrea Funk owns Too Cool T-shirt Quilts, Inc. in Charlotte, Michigan. Her company makes about 1,000 T-shirt quilts every year. Before I started making the Warm Memories T-Shirt Quilt, I asked her for some top-notch advice. She said:

- "It's a fairly common misconception that T-shirt materials *must* be stabilized with fusible interfacing before they can be sewn into a quilt. It's true that if you are *mixing* woven quilting cottons with knitted T-shirt materials, the T-shirt should be stabilized. However, if you are sewing T-shirt to T-shirt, it's not necessary to stabilize the T-shirts.
- When cutting the T-shirt, be careful to avoid adding any tension to the material. For example, if you place the T-shirt on your cutting mat, stretch it, then cut it. The T-shirt will relax back to its prestretched shape, which is not likely to be the size and shape you intended. Also, be aware that T-shirts have a right and a wrong side.
- Once cut, the T-shirt will curl along the sides. Don't be alarmed! This is normal behavior for knit material. When the T-shirt is pieced, the curl will not affect the quilt.
- When piecing T-shirts, use a walking foot or even feed foot.
- T-shirts are lint factories. Be kind to your sewing machine with frequent cleaning while your T-shirt quilt is under construction.
- Before fusing stabilizing interfacing to the back of any T-shirt, check the label for fiber content. Test a small section of the T-shirt to make sure it won't melt.
- Experiment first. Buy some plain T-shirts at the discount store or purchase them at a garage sale and try cutting and piecing them. A few test seams will give you confidence before cutting into your impossible-to-replace favorites.
- Don't hand-quilt a T-shirt quilt. Machine quilting a T-shirt quilt can be tricky. Perhaps the best approach is to tie a T-shirt quilt."

The Not-So-Secret Language of Quilters

Like a secret handshake between BFFs, quilters have their own special code. Pick any social gathering: If more than one quilter is in attendance, they find each other. Call it a common thread. An eerie coincidence. Kismet. Or the telltale errant thread stuck to your jacket. In a heartbeat, the conversation turns to quilting, baffling our spouses and significant others.

The following collection of terms (some more whimsical than others) will support your next quilty gab session.

Apple core block: A curved block that looks like a circle with a bite taken out of two sides. When placed side by side, and rotated 90 degrees, the blocks appear to interlock.

Appliqué: A quilt-making technique that involves sewing shapes made from fabric to a base fabric to create a motif or block.

Basting thread: Cotton thread that breaks away easily. Basting thread is suitable for securing the quilt sandwich for quilting. Basting thread is especially nice because quilting stitches may split the basting thread. The basting thread will break away easily without damaging the quilt or the quilting stitches.

Betweens: As in *quilting* betweens. A shorter, sturdier needle used to hand-quilt.

Big-stitch quilting: A method to secure the quilt sandwich with pearl cotton. The stitches are generally much larger (one stitch per ¼ in.) than traditional heirloom quilting (10 stitches per inch).

Blanket stitch: A decorative stitch that can be made by hand or machine. The blanket or buttonhole stitch consists of straight stitches alternated with perpendicular stitches. It's commonly used to secure machine appliqué pieces to a background fabric.

Chain piecing: A piecing method whereby fabric shapes are sewn one after the next with two or three empty stitches in between.

Crazy quilting: A traditional piecing style that combines a variety of fabric types and decorative embroidery stitches, typically done by hand.

Crosshairs: A hand-quilting term used to describe where the seamlines meet. The seamlines are the stitching lines drawn on the wrong side of the fabric.

Decorative stitch: All those cool stitches on the sewing machine that you never use because you are too busy using the straight stitch for piecing and quilting.

Domestic sewing machine: The type of sewing machine used by most home sewists. It may be placed in a cabinet or on a tabletop while in use. It is often stored under the kitchen table and pulled out immediately after the dinner table has been cleared for evening/early-morning quilting sessions. Also, the source of envy at quilt retreat weekends when a discussion ensues over who has the most domestic sewing machines in their collection.

Double backstitch: A backstitch is a stitch on top of the last stitch to lock the threads in place. A double backstitch is two stitches on top of the last stitch to really secure the thread.

Downside of the seam: My way of saying where to place the line of stitching for in-the-ditch quilting. Look for the seam, then feel the bulk of the seam. The side of the seam without the seam allowance is the downside of the seam.

Edgestitch: A line of straight stitches along the edge of a quilt or rim of a bag. An edgestitch compresses the bulk at the fabric edge. See also *topstitch*.

Even feed or integrated foot: I also call it dual feed. A built-in attachment on a sewing machine that advances the fabric under the needle from the top while the feed dogs advance the fabric from the bottom.

Fabric real estate: Fabric, basically. The more real estate you have, the better.

Feed dogs: These puppies don't bark. They are the little jagged ridges in the sewing machine bed that advance the fabric away from you as you sew.

Float: The addition of extra fabric, as in setting triangles, so that the corners or points of the block or block elements won't be jeopardized when borders or additional fabrics are added.

Flying geese unit: A block element named after the V-formation made by geese flying south for the winter. Coincidentally, the block element named after the V-formation made by geese flying north for the summer is also called a flying geese unit.

Furl: Also called *popping* or *spinning* the seam. The process of opening the center seam intersection and rotating the pressing direction so the seams rotate around the intersection. I use this term a lot because I furl a lot.

Fussy-cut: The process of cutting fabric for a quilt block or quilt block element based on the placement of printed illustrations or motifs on that fabric. When fussy-cutting, it's important to take into account the seam allowances. Also, a very expensive haircut.

Grading: Remove a small amount (about $1/16$ in.) of the seam allowance after piecing. This will keep the darker seams from showing through on the right side of the quilt. It also creates a gradual slope for a smoother hand-quilting experience. Just be careful that you don't cut straight through the seam allowance to the pieced element. Then you'll experience *repairing* instead of *grading*.

Half-square triangle (HST): Otherwise known as, in mathematical terms, an isosceles right triangle. The

straight of grain typically follows the shorter sides of the triangle, and the hypotenuse follows the fabric bias. The quick-and-dirty formula to cut the mathematically correct HST is to take the finished size of the HST unit, then add $7/8$ in.; cut a square, then cut it in half once along the diagonal.

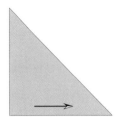

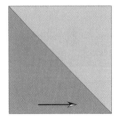

Half-square triangle unit (HST unit): A square quilt block or quilt block element made from two HSTs sewn along the hypotenuses.

Hexagon: A six-sided quilt shape. Related: 90-degree hexagon, half-hexagon, quarter hexagon, etc.

In-the-ditch quilting: Sewing through all the layers of a quilt sandwich along the seam allowance.

Ladder stitch: A method to close a seam by hand. Thread the needle and insert it within the seam allowance on one side of the opening, pass the needle through the seam allowance on the opposite side of the opening, and continue to work from side to side across the opening until it is secure.

LQS (Local Quilt Shop): (1) A fun place to buy fabric and notions for quilting. (2) A live, in-person help-desk for quilt geeks. (3) A currency exchange outlet—you bring money, and the LQS exchanges it for currency that is measured by the yard.

Match-marks: Especially in hand-piecing, a tick-mark placed on the seamline so two pieces of fabric can be aligned partway across a seam for sewing.

Meander: A quilting pattern characterized by loopy, wavy lines that resemble Mickey Mouse fingers or winding country roads.

Miter: 45-degree seams or folds in a 90-degree corner, as in *mitered borders* or *mitered binding corners*.

Monofilament thread: Uncoated single-ply synthetic thread.

Needle clamp: The bolt that sticks out from the needle bar that holds the needle in place on the sewing machine.

Needle down: The opposite of needle up. A sewing machine setting that automatically sets the sewing machine needle at the lowest position when you stop sewing.

Needle plate: The metal plate that covers the bobbin case. Or, the sewing machine's "belly button": Remove this to get the lint out!

Needle up: The opposite of needle down. A sewing machine setting that automatically sets the sewing machine needle at the highest position when you stop sewing.

Nest: (1) The place where a mother bird lays her eggs. (2) The point where seams that have been pressed in opposite directions intersect with minimal bulk. (3) The unsightly bunch of knotted and twisted threads formed on the wrong side of the stitching that cannot be removed by even the most patient quilter.

Orphan quilt blocks: If you are a new quilter, just wait a while. You'll have lots of these. You get them when you fall out of love with a quilt after you've made a few blocks.

Pinwheel block: Four HST units sewn together in a four-patch in an alternating dark/light value progression. The resulting quilt block resembles a child's pinwheel toy.

Pressing direction: Turning both layers of the seam allowance to one side, often identified by a little arrow in a quilt pattern illustration.

Quarter-square triangle (QST): A piece of square fabric cut in half on both diagonals. Like a HST, this

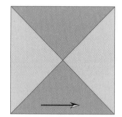

is also an isosceles right triangle. In this case, the straight of grain usually follows the longest side or the hypotenuse. The quick-and-dirty formula to cut the mathematically correct QST is to take the finished size of the longest side of the QST unit, then add 1¼ in.; cut a square, then cut it in half along both diagonals.

Quarter-square triangle unit (QST unit): A square quilt block or quilt block element made from four QSTs sewn so all the 90-degree angles meet in the middle of the block.

Quilt sandwich: Backing, batting, and quilt top, layered and basted.

Quilting: (1) The process of making the best kind of comforter known to humankind by cutting up perfectly good large pieces of fabric into smaller pieces, then sewing the smaller pieces of fabric together to make a big piece of fabric that is then layered with batting and backing, then quilted. (2) A socially acceptable excuse to ignore any other type of menial task, like cleaning.

Quilty: It's not really a word, but it should be, because it's so much fun to say.

Right sides together: Putting the pretty sides of the fabric together, with the fabric edge aligned to sew the seam.

Scant quarter inch: A thread width (or two) less than ¼ in.

Seam allowance: The part of the fabric you don't see. In quilting, the seam allowance is typically ¼ in.

Seam intersection: The point where more than two seams come together to form a point or corner.

Seam ripper: The most frequently used tool in a sewist's tool kit. Commonly, its use is immediately preceded by not-very-nice language from the user.

Seamed horizontally: I use this term frequently when referring to the backing fabric when the seam runs horizontally, along the shorter dimension of the quilt. More typically, a backing seam is vertical, but a horizontal seam may minimize waste.

Secondary patterns: Patterns that "show up" when quilt blocks are placed next to each other.

Set-in seam: A Y-seam, for example. Then, of course, there's the Y-knot . . . gotcha!

Sewist: One who sews. I prefer to refer to myself as a sewist. If you'd like to be called a sewer, that's fine, but personally, I think that's kinda stinky.

Shadowing: Dark seams that show through lighter fabrics.

Slipstitch: A hand stitch used to secure the fold of the binding to the back of the quilt or to secure appliqué shapes by hand.

Stash: (1) Fabric folded neatly on the shelf waiting to be selected for a quilt project. (2) Fabric still in the shopping bag, usually with the receipt removed and burned to eliminate all evidence of procurement price and date. (3) Fabric wadded up in baskets, bags, or any horizontal surface in your home and sewing studio. (4) Fabric stored under the bed, in the car trunk, or at your neighbor's house so that it can be brought into your sewing studio in small, reasonable quantities. (5) A measurement unit, i.e., your stash is bigger than/smaller than your quilty friend's. (6) A type of retirement investment savings account, like an IRA, but in bright colors that you can touch and fold over and over again.

Straight stitch: A sewing machine stitch that has length but no width. The stitch length can be adjusted for various types of piecing, quilting, or basting.

Strip-piece: Sewing strips together that have been cut the full width-of-fabric to make strip-sets. Often the strip-sets are then cross-cut into smaller pieces.

Strip-set: Two or more width-of-fabric strips of fabric sewn together side by side along the cut edge. See *strip-piece*.

Topstitch: A straight or decorative stitch that compresses a fabric fold. Also see *edgestitch*.

Topper: A quilter who stops when the quilt top is complete. He or she often does the quilting "with his/her checkbook," if at all. *Wink, wink.*

Traditionally pieced borders: Borders that are added to the quilt center one at a time.

True-up: As in true-up a quilt block. Take a ruler, measure the block, and hack off any extra stuff. I much prefer to figure out why the block is out-of-size before hacking away at it. I reserve my violent tendencies for the block elements.

Tumbler blocks: Trapezoidally shaped quilt blocks, typically sewn together in rows.

UFO: (1) An obsession for many quilters; also known as UnFinished Objects or Projects Half Done (PhD), may be tracked by complex multilayer spreadsheets. (2) A measurement unit, see also *stash*.

Variegated thread: Multicolored thread that comes off one spool. Often used for quilting.

Width-of-fabric: The selvage-to-selvage fabric dimension, typically 40 in. to 42 in.

Y-seam: Where three pieces of fabric intersect at something other than 90-degree or 180-degree angles.

Zigzag stitch: Had to throw this in to include the last letter of the alphabet! A straight stitch with a stitch width that is greater than 0. The zigzag stitch is popular for securing machine appliqué or stabilizing raw edges on the inside of a bag, for example.

Resources

Quilters Dream Batting
Single-sided fusible batting for T-shirt quilt
www.quiltersdreambatting.com

Quiltsmart, Inc.
Printed fusible interfacing for T-shirt quilt
www.quiltsmart.com

Lazy Girl Designs
Face-it Firm or Face-it Soft interfacing
www.lazygirldesigns.com

Inklingo
Shapes and instructions for printing stitching lines
on fabric for hand piecing
www.lindafranz.com

Joyful Adornments by Bonnie
Glass buttons, beads, and other adornments for
your quilts
www.joyfuladornments.com

Contributors

Susan K. Cleveland
www.piecesbewithyou.com

Pepper Cory
www.peppercory.com

Carolyn Friedlander
www.carolynfriedlander.com

Andrea Funk
www.toocooltshirtquilts.com

Rhonda Pierce
Marketing Director, Euro-Notions and
www.Schmetzneedles.com

Sharon Stroud
www.sharonstroud.com

Tom West
Swiss-Trained Technician, Patchwork Plus Quilt Shop,
Marcellus, New York

Index